Certify & Sell

Your Guide to Certification & Supplier Diversity

By Joanne E. Peterson

With Marian E. Neilson

Sager Brown Publishing

Pittsburgh, PA

CERTIFY & SELL: YOUR GUIDE TO CERTIFICATION & SUPPLIER DIVERSITY

Printed in the United States of America

ISBN: 978-0-578-81651-7

Cover design by Tara Phillips
Edited by Cori Wamsley

In Memory of Andrew S. Neilson

Table of Contents

Introduction

You wouldn't necessarily think growing up in 1960s Pittsburgh, Pa., would lead to a passion for supplier diversity. Steel was king, electricity queen, and we had a royal family of metals, chemicals, and education. The city was so full of science and industry in general that it made us the third largest city in the country for corporate headquarters —U.S. Steel, Westinghouse, Alcoa, and Gulf Oil were based here while Jonas Salk conquered polio with his vaccine.

Joanne's father, an Ohio transplant, served in World War II and graduated from Carnegie Tech (now Carnegie Mellon University) in 1946. He was employed in the steel industry, initially as a metallurgical engineer, making rolls. As a child, she thought that meant "biscuits" when, in reality, these were immense components to roll out huge sheets of steel for various applications. He was full of stories about the plant, and his children got to know most of his ethnically diverse coworkers at the company picnics and Christmas parties.

"It is the policy of the government of the United States to provide equal opportunity in federal employment for all persons, to prohibit discrimination in employment because of race, color, religion, sex, national origin, handicap, age, sexual orientation, or status as a parent, and to promote the full realization of equal employment opportunity through a continuing affirmative program in each executive department and agency. This policy of equal opportunity applies to and must be an integral part of every aspect of personnel policy and practice in the employment, development, advancement, and treatment of civilian employees of the federal government, to the extent permitted by law."

(Nixon R. M., 1969)

Coming of age during the late 1960s and early 1970s meant participating with friends of all colors in the upheaval associated with the Civil Rights movement. President Kennedy's funeral procession and the assassinations of Dr. King and Senator Kennedy made indelible pictures in the minds of those watching in real time, and we believed, with Dr. King's dream, that we could overcome anything with enough love and kindness for each other. But what one believes at 11 or 12 required decades of hard work that continues to demand our best efforts to achieve.

The stories changed as the 1960s marched into the 1970s. Joanne and her friends lived through the visions of the 1968–69 riots after Dr. King's murder—Washington, Chicago, Baltimore, and Cleveland (where she was in 1968)—and came out the other side to sit-ins and peaceful marches, at least on her college campus in Boston, where they succeeded in establishing a black[1] student union.

In this heavily unionized blue-collar town, affirmative action had a big impact. Pennsylvania, and the Pittsburgh area specifically, has always been a multi-cultural community. Our schools were desegregated in 1875 and in 1887 our first black council member was elected (Popular Pittsburgh, 2016). Jobs, opportunities, and jazz beckoned; between 1910 and 1930, a large migration of African American families arrived in Pittsburgh from the rural South. In the late 1950s and early 1960s, Pittsburgh destroyed the vibrant lower Hill District with Renaissance One. This was an area inhabited predominantly by people of African descent, and it was demolished to build what was the Civic Arena complex[2]. This

---

[1] The terms "African American," "Asian American," "Hispanic American," "Native American," and "people of color" had yet to be coined.

[2] The Civic Arena, later named the Mellon Arena, opened in 1961 and was torn down in 2011–12.

Certify and Sell

short-sighted mistake cleared 95 acres and displaced thousands of people and hundreds of small businesses. Then, affirmative action came along and required that Pittsburgh's largest employers, and the related unions, expand their commitments to its African American citizens.

Chapter 1: History of Certification

President Harry S. Truman once said, "We can tolerate no restrictions upon the individual which depend upon irrelevant factors such as *his* race, *his* color, *his* religion, or the social position to which *he* is born." (The Report of the President's Committee on Civil Rights, 1946) We chose to emphasize "his" here because, although female suffrage had won us the right to vote in 1920 (National Archives, 1920), we women weren't often included in the early language about affirmative action or diversity. It wasn't until 1971 that President Nixon amended the rules that affirmative action began to include women (Nixon R. M., Executive Order 11625, 1971). Today, the Equal Employment Opportunity Commission (EEOC) oversees the federal objective of equal employment opportunities for all.

Supplier diversity has its roots in 1964's Civil Rights and Affirmative Action legislation. President Johnson's September 24, 1965 (Executive Order 11246) established the Office of Federal Contract Compliance. This required companies with federal contracts to make good-faith efforts to expand employment opportunities for both women and minorities. Once large corporations were required to comply with EEOC and the rules established as a result of legal actions taken throughout the country, supplier diversity became the next logical step. In fact, President Nixon used an executive order to create the federal Office of Minority Business Enterprise (OMBE) (Exectuive Order 11458, 1969).

In 1971, President Nixon issued another order (Executive Order 11625), directing federal agencies to develop comprehensive plans and specific program goals for a national Minority Business Enterprise (MBE[3]) contracting program. The Small Business Act of 1953 was amended to require "... all federal contracts in excess of $150,000 dollars provide maximum practicable opportunity for small and small disadvantaged business to participate and that all those in excess of $650,000 dollars ($1,500,000 dollars in the case of construction contracts for public facilities) be accompanied by a formal subcontracting plan containing separate goals for small business and small disadvantaged business." (Congress, H.R.11318 , 1978) Then, President Reagan issued an executive order, which directed each federal agency with substantial procurement or grant making authority to develop a Minority Business Enterprise (MBE) development plan (Executive

---

[3] Like many fields, certification has lots of jargon. Check out Appendix Glossary for a comprehensive list.

Order 12432, 1983). In 1979, the agency was renamed the Minority Business Development Agency (MBDA), and it is now a part of the U.S. Department of Commerce.

The actions of Presidents Kennedy, Johnson, Nixon, and Reagan led to the formal process of identifying and vetting the credentials of businesses that claim to be owned and operated by qualified members of diverse ethnicity, veterans', woman's, or disabled groups. This process is what we call "diversity certification."

The Department of Transportation (DOT) and three of its operating programs—the Federal Highway Administration, the Federal Aviation Administration and the Federal Transit Administration—were tasked with implementing the program nationwide. The policies and procedures the agency developed became the foundation for every state government certification, with a twist ... the individual state organizations applied their own modifications. It happened enough that a Montana official once commented "... it is one program with 53 implementations." (Peterson, 2013) Then, the third-party certifiers, who have adapted the same process, came along. No matter who you choose to get certified by, this is how the hoops you'll jump through came to be.

CMS ILLINOIS
DEPARTMENT OF
CENTRAL MANAGEMENT SERVICES

Eugene S. Reineke, Director

Rose Mary Bombela, Assistant Director
Daniel R. Long, Assistant Director

ABATOR INFORMATION SERVICES
1601 PENN AVENUE
SUITE 602
PITTSBURGH, PA   15221

OCTOBER 17, 1989

DEAR VENDOR:

THANK YOU FOR RETURNING YOUR COMPLETED BIDDER'S APPLICATION FORM. BASED ON THE INFORMATION PROVIDED, THE NAME OF YOUR FIRM HAS BEEN PLACED ON THE DEPARTMENT OF CENTRAL MANAGEMENT SERVICES' BID LIST FOR COMMODITIES, GENERAL EQUIPMENT AND SUPPLIES.

WE HAVE CLASSIFIED THE FIRM YOU REPRESENT AS A LARGE BUSINESS THAT IS FEMALE OWNED.

ALL PROCUREMENTS OF COMMODITIES, EQUIPMENT AND SUPPLIES CONFORM TO THE REQUIREMENTS OF THE ENCLOSED "STANDARD PROCUREMENT RULES." YOU ARE URGED TO READ AND BECOME FAMILIAR WITH THIS PUBLICATION.

ALTHOUGH YOU ARE ON THE DEPARTMENT OF CENTRAL MANAGEMENT SERVICES' BID LIST, THERE ARE CERTAIN PROCUREMENTS THAT ARE NOT AUTOMATICALLY SENT BIDS BASED ON THIS VENDOR LIST. THIS APPLIES GENERALLY TO SERVICES OF ALL TYPES, INCLUDING CONSTRUCTION, AND PROCUREMENTS OF SPECIALIZED EQUIPMENT SUCH AS DATA PROCESSING AND TELECOMMUNICATIONS EQUIPMENT. IN ORDER TO BE AWARE OF THESE PROCUREMENTS, IT IS NECESSARY TO MONITOR THE LEGAL ADVERTISEMENTS IN THE OFFICIAL STATE NEWSPAPER AND REQUEST A COPY OF THE RELEVANT INVITATION FOR BIDS OR REQUEST FOR PROPOSALS IN ACCORDANCE WITH INSTRUCTIONS IN THE ADVERTISEMENT.

THE OFFICIAL STATE NEWSPAPER IS CURRENTLY THE KEWANEE STAR COURIER, LEGAL ADVERTISING, 105 EAST CENTRAL BOULEVARD, KEWANEE, ILLINOIS 61443 (309/852-0010). THE ANNUAL SUBSCRIPTION COST IS $129.75. THE OFFICIAL STATE NEWSPAPER IS SELECTED ON AN ANNUAL BASIS AND MAY CHANGE BEGINNING JULY 1 OF EACH YEAR.

YOU SHOULD ALSO NOTE THAT SMALL PROCUREMENTS, GENERALLY THOSE LESS THAN $5,000, MIGHT BE ADVERTISED IN A LOCAL NEWSPAPER IN LIEU OF THE OFFICIAL STATE NEWSPAPER, IF THE AGENCY BELIEVES THE NEED CAN BE FILLED LOCALLY.

IF YOU HAVE QUESTIONS REGARDING THIS LETTER, PLEASE CALL ME AT 217/785-3900.

SINCERELY,

R. L. Henrikson

R. L. HENRIKSON
COORDINATOR OF SPECIFICATIONS,
COMPLIANCE AND TRAINING

ENC.

RLH:RW:4546Y

VENDOR NO: 45676

801 Stratton Office Building, Springfield, Illinois 62706

Founded in April 1983, our business was a WBE (Women Business Enterprise), WOSB (Women-Owned Small Business) and DOBE (Disabled Owned Business) before these acronyms existed! The business existed before Reagan's order required federal agencies to establish spending goals for contracts (Reagan, 1983).

In Our Certification Beginning

In the late 1980s, we had a consultant who had traveled extensively on our behalf completing engagements with clients like RJR/Nabisco, Boeing/McDonnell Douglas, and Westinghouse among others. Wayne asked if we'd make an effort to find him an engagement closer to his home base in central Illinois. An Illinois request for proposals was on the street at the time, so we decided in our naiveté to pursue a state master services contract. Before we knew what certification was, we won an award in September of 1989, and as part of the contract paperwork, we were required to fill out a form about the ownership and sales history of the company. We reported the previous three years of sales figures, with a breakdown of the outstanding stock, and a list of our board of directors. Surprisingly, a few weeks later, we received our first ever certification that named Abator a large[4] FBE (female business enterprise). We promptly filed it with the rest of the legalese and went about building teams that developed social

---

[4] Not part of the DOT program, states can often apply different size standards. In those days, sales over million dollars indicated a large business.

service type applications in support of Illinois' citizens. Illinois was our first government customer to ask us to provide that kind of information.

Predominantly involved in commercial development or technical support on large mainframes around the country, IBM was an elephantine client we chased for a decade until finally landing a contract in 1996. During said chase, IBM was the first commercial client to ask us about our ownership in 1986. We completed a slew of paperwork to qualify as a potential vendor, and one of those pages was very similar to the Illinois form.

If you look at IBM's Supplier Diversity web pages, you'll discover its program really began with its 1968 procurement practices, long before the legislation or MBDA existed. At the time, we spoke at length with Sherri Robison while trying to understand what IBM expected from its suppliers, completing forms (on an IBM Selectric II typewriter, pre-email, pre-PDF era) about the technical skills our teams could provide. We met up with Sherri many times over the years, while a supplier and after. We often spoke with her about diversity issues, especially at conferences around the country.

Women's Business Enterprise Certification

This is to certify that

Abator Information Services, Inc.
Information Technology Consultant
SIC Code(s): 7370, 7371, 7373

Has successfully met the eligibility criteria for certification as a bona fide
Women's Business Enterprise
and is enrolled as a WBE in

The Ohio Women's Business Development Council, Inc.,
a partner in the network of certifying organizations with the

Women's Business Enterprise National Council,
and that applies standards and procedures adopted by the WBENC board of directors.

Certification Number: 0534
Date of Certification: 09/14/99
Expiration Date: 09/13/02

Linda Steward,
President

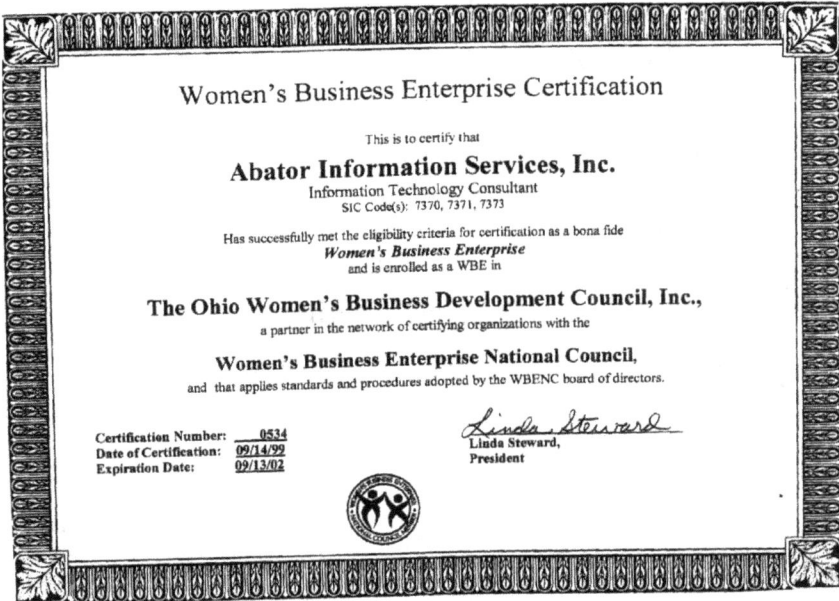

As the world prepared for potential Y2K[5] doom, we won a contract with Ohio's Jobs & Family Services agency. They asked us to complete a lot of contract-related paperwork, including several pages for their certifier of WBEs. It only took three clients to make us understand that Minority and Women Business Enterprises (MWBE) certification was a thing that they cared about.

It was through Ohio's request we became familiar with and joined the Women's Business Enterprise National Council

---

[5] See Appendix Y2K and the Projected Death of COBOL

(WBENC) in 1999. We celebrated our 20-year anniversary with WBENC in 2019.

With our offices in Pennsylvania and Missouri, certifying with agencies in these states made logical sense to us. Then, we started seeing two patterns: 1) that we had built up significant expertise in state government contracting; and, 2) that most of our clients actually cared that we were women-owned and operated. We bit the bullet and filed our first DOT-based Disadvantaged Business Enterprise (DBE) application with Allegheny County[6] several years before today's Unified Certification Programs began. By the time 2003 was over, we held WBE certifications from Pennsylvania's PennDOT, WBENC, and Allegheny County. In 2004, we added New York, Rhode Island, and Maryland certificates. Mid-2020, we're the proud holders of multiple certifications: over 28 state, 2 third-party, and 1 federal.

What started as a single page form had become virtual projects of their own with a mandatory almost new application package every third year and annual affidavits of no change. While state DOT organizations had similar forms, they each had special requirements, differing questions, or different

---

[6] See Appendix County 2002 Application Redacted

supporting documentation. Non-DOT agencies and third-party certifiers had comparable core information requests, extra questions, and different document requirements. Like most new and small businesses, we had an entrepreneurial dream that certainly did NOT include learning how to deal with bureaucratic forms and processes far outside our primary business day. We're also IT folks, so we developed internal systems to manage and support our certification application process. This became GetDiversityCertified.com. If you're unfamiliar with the hoops a business jumps through to acquire and maintain certification, the FAQS page and our blog is full of information. We love to educate about certification from the supplier's point of view.

There were some interesting hurdles to clear along the way. Experiences taught us that certifiers' processes can be subjective. As IT aficionados we understand the value of solving the same problem (anti-fraudulent certification) with similar procedures (forms, supporting documents) and personal verifications (site visits). But we found we were trying to comply with programs and forms that were just different enough that *paperwork nightmare* became an accurate description of our early experiences. The forms alone grew to a current high of 15 pages for the state DOT DBE programs[7]. A full application for a relatively small but older company like ours with two recently deceased owners with stock transfers across two generations and seven related current owners, three of whom have another small business that owns our office space, means roughly 45 pages of forms to fill out.

Often, though they arrive electronically, the forms are locked (or protected) so people can't fill them out with a document editor. One state employee claimed that it was so we couldn't change the form. Ever the techies, we scanned it, added text and check box controls to complete it in a manner more comfortable for us.

Some forms wanted the owner's name in a single box, while others had two boxes for first and last. A limited number had separate codes to describe a person's ethnicity, so the responder has to look up an identification abbreviation that aligns. Of course, Caucasian (white American) is not always listed, so it must be entered manually. Many applications' page one led with a question about the relationship between the owners of the business two to four pages before it asked who the owners were. Most states want a completed personal net

---

[7] See Appendix for Sample DOT DBE Form

worth statement from the disadvantaged owner(s) only. A few want it from owners with more than 10% ownership position, while other states want it from each owner. Since the personal net worth statement is a three-page form, we could be producing anywhere from three to fifteen form pages of personal net worth alone.

The required documents vary little between certifiers: owner resumes that describe what you do in and for your business and financial reports, complete with business tax returns and often personal returns. Though most programs recognize permanent resident applications, some certifiers will only certify businesses owned by U.S. citizens (born here or naturalized), so a birth certificate or passport for the diverse owner(s) is necessary.

For government certifications, business size standards must be met, which have changed a lot since 1989. Back then, "small" for us was an annual sales volume under $1.5 million. In 2020, the size standards based on the North American Industry Codes (NAICS) require our averaged annual sales[8] to be below $30.0 million. Whether a business meets the "small"

---

[8] Average annual sales are calculated by the most recent five years added together then divided by five. Prior to 6 January 2020 the average annual sales were calculated using the most recent three years of sales.

designation is determined by Congress and the Small Business Administration (SBA).

The Small Business Act of 1953 gave SBA authority to establish size standards, and there are currently four measures: number of employees, average annual sales as reported in the last five years, average asset size reported in previous four quarters, and the mystifying "combination of number of employees and barrel per day refining capacity." After the initial standards were set in 1957, the SBA occasionally made changes to the standards by looking at individual industries, usually at the request of legislators who believed market conditions had changed for a particular segment of business. Complicated formulas are used that are way beyond our scope or understanding. (Dilger, 2019)

As a business seeking small and/or disadvantaged certification, the best way to find out the size standard for your business is to visit the SBA's website (Small Business Administration (SBA), 2019). The information tends to be in a spreadsheet with the first column containing NAICS code and the second a very brief description, followed by columns containing the criteria for size by millions of dollars and/or number of employees. NAICS codes are interesting, because the list continues to grow and a business could have more than one or two (we have eight). For businesses unsure of the appropriate NAICS code, there is a key word-based search function available at the U.S. Census website. (Executive Office of the President OMB, 2016)

None of the programs can completely eliminate subjective analysis or interpretation of any given application package. Remember, Abator has always been at or above 71% women-owned and operated. One certifier decided that substantial loans from a male director gave him power over the board of directors, though. Another required us to provide literally 32 years' worth of shareholder and director meeting minutes . . . even our home state only asked for first and most recent. We agreed, provided we could submit an electronic copy. Who would want to print and ship what amounted to another 251 pages, anyway? We often wonder if anyone read them. Bad news, it took two people two days to scan all those pages. Good news, all of our history is digitally backed up. This same state came back and told us we were likely to be denied because a recent death changed the composition of our board. We'll never understand how they came to interpret our corporation's bylaws to one person equals one vote, rather than our entire existence of one share equals one vote and she with the most shares wins. Our next call was to the attorney to amend those bylaws, preventing any future misinterpretation.

Certify and Sell

In July 2018, the SBA pointed out that our primary NAICS wasn't on our 2017 corporate tax return[9]. Yes, the next letter went to the CPA. The first thing we looked at on our 2018 return was our NAICS code – verifying that the correct code was now in use.

Finally, there's the question of proving ethnicity. Because, believe it not, limited progress has been made, you won't find race on a northern state birth certificate after the late 1800s or southern ones after the 1960s. But, to claim minority status, the diverse owner is required to prove they are at least 25% ethnic minority. That means if neither you nor your parents have race listed on your birth certificates, at least one of your grandparents must. If not, then you'll need to find some official school, state, tribal or formal church document that shows the disadvantaged owner(s) are at least 25% non-Caucasian, or there may be a problem.

Think DNA testing would suffice? When we surveyed a few agencies, we found there are differing perspectives on DNA results. One agency would accept reports from Ancestry or 23&Me to prove 25% ethnicity, while another scoffed at the

_____

[9] Just two weeks after the June 2018 SBA's OIG report on improperly WOSB awarded contracts became public.

idea. One said their agency would award certification if the owner looked African-American. We expect this will become a hotly debated issue as we get further removed from race on birth certificates because looks can certainly be deceiving.

Then there were the agencies that wanted other documentation. A copy of a divorce decree—even though the ex-husband referenced never had an ownership position. Resumes and tax returns for all owners (not just the disadvantaged ones), which led to a phone conversation about what to submit for very young children whose stock is being voted by their paternal aunt, also an owner in the business. Tongue in cheek, we offered finger-painted art with Polaroid photos. They accepted copies of birth certificates, the stock certificates and ledger (that listed who was voting their shares), and a signed, notarized letter that these two young boys weren't making critical control or governance decisions for the company. Yet another required notarized statements on what contributions these children made to acquire their stock, even though the ledger clearly documented that they had inherited shares from their great-grandfather and great-aunt—not an unusual scenario in a family-owned business.

We've learned so much—one of us has a 300-page living document covering every diversity-based certification she can find. Then people started asking us to help them. We began offering training and other assistance to other small and medium businesses looking to travel the certification path. Our first blog item was published in August of 2010, introducing ourselves. We found our next post a "Short History of Supplier Diversity" referenced in the back of Scott Vowels' 2017 book *Hacking Supplier Diversity*. (Vowels P. S., 2017) The blog continues, joined by Twitter and LinkedIn accounts.

While building an automated system with 12,000 rules to collect and evaluate business information and documents for 250+ certifying agencies, we engaged with Chatham University's Center for Women's Entrepreneurship and its Women's Business Center to deliver a workshop we call *Am I Certifiable?* Most of that material is covered in the next few chapters, but the real value has been the interactive nature of these Q&A sessions. New questions or a different way of asking them, educates us every time.

As diverse business owners, we've been beneficiaries of the work done by activists and politicians to level the playing field for us. We believe in *walking the walk* and in *paying it forward*, supporting members of our vast community. Abator always seeks other certified companies to partner with in the pursuit of large government contracts, whether we are required to or not. The continued growth of certified diverse businesses will have a positive impact on the U.S. economy and help grow the number of jobs available. These businesses will solve existing problems, develop new products and create things we might not even be able to imagine today. Let us give the history, explain why and show them how to take advantage of our knowledge to get their businesses certified.

Chapter 2: Why Certify

We get frequent calls from semi-panicked business owners whose client has just asked if they're a certified diverse business. A surprising number of them ask us what that means; many think they qualify as MBE or WBE or veteran business enterprise (VBE); a lesser number know about LGBTBE (lesbian-, gay-, bi-sexual-, or transgender-owned) or DOBE (disabled-owned) certification opportunities. The conversation begins to look and feel like one of our programs as one of us explains the definitions:

- Diverse Business: must be at least 51% owned, operated, governed, and controlled by U.S. minorities[10] or women. This designation could also include people with a disability, with veteran or service-disabled veteran status, or who are lesbian, gay, bisexual, or transgender, depending on the certifying agency in question.

---

[10] For information on international minority definitions, check out Chapter 20 International Certifiers

- Certification: formal review process designed so only firms that meet eligibility criteria obtain certified status.

Certification is actually a co-dependent relationship. The business is being certified as having the capability to provide its products and/or services, and its diverse owner(s) must possess the knowledge and skill to run the business. This means that the business's diversity certification is reliant on its owner(s)! And, we have to know how to get the work that falls under our NAICS code(s).

Abator's primary codes are 541512, Computer Systems Design Service, "primarily engaged in planning and designing computer systems that integrate computer hardware, software, and communication technologies," or 541511, Custom Computer Programming Service, "primarily engaged in writing, modifying, testing, and supporting software to meet the needs of a particular client." This means that the owners of our business need to able to plan, design, and implement software either personally or have the skills to identify and manage the staff that does.

Did you notice the words "governed" or "controlled" in the description for a diversity business? The thing is, just because the owners might meet the designation and percentage of ownership doesn't mean they have been given the power or authority to govern and control the business. "Governance" boils down to the language in the governing documents[11] of the business, and certifiers will make sure that there are no restrictions on the diverse owner's ability to control the business, while "control" means the diverse owner(s) must have the authority and "power to direct or determine" or influence what will happen in the business, both now and in the future.

When it comes to control, there are two pretty simple conditions that must be met by the diverse owner(s):

- Financial control: the owner's signature on bank documents or contracts with the bank or other creditors and business credit cards bearing the owner's name and signature with a history of significant business-related purchases.

- Management control: negotiation of and the owner's signature on contracts with customers and vendors; hiring and firing decisions, including performance

---

[11] Each type of business structure has its own type of governing documents.

evaluations; supervision of business operations; office management; entering into lease or property agreements; marketing and sales; and purchasing major equipment.

Management control is usually straight forward: the diverse owner must be seen executing the responsibilities that they have been authorized to handle, either by themselves or directing others who perform tasks. Governance can be tricky. The diverse owner must have the title that is considered the highest leadership role, generally something like "president," "CEO," "chairperson," or "managing partner/member." In the business's managing documents, such as bylaws or operating agreement, the diverse owner must have the responsibilities to go with it, such as diverse owner(s) must have executive power over the affairs and property of the business, power to carry out policies and programs, all powers of the office, and the power to execute deeds, bonds, mortgages, other contracts, agreements, and other legal instruments. They must also perform all duties of the office.

A business with a single owner should be easy, right? As a sole proprietor, perhaps, but with the highly popular one-person limited liability company (LLC), an operating agreement is required and the diverse owner's title and executive role must be explicitly defined.

Don't save money on legal advice if you want to be a certified diverse business. Your second cousin practicing family law probably doesn't know every twist in language that might affect an owner's ability to get their business certified. A business law or civil attorney is a good investment, and a business owner ought to make sure that the lawyer understands what they want regarding certification status.

Owners need to read and re-read those documents carefully, asking questions about anything not completely understood. You will find a ton of legalese throughout, but any of us should be able to recognize some of the phrasing. For example, if the business has a 51/49 split in ownership, there should be no language that indicates *equal* risk and reward, and the word "unanimous" should not appear!

To be certified, that 51% risk and 51% share of any rewards is a key to the diverse owner's ability to get certified. Any arrangement that has the diverse person not owning and controlling the lion's share (51% minimum) of the business is unlikely to be certifiable. And, the 51% owner should have larger contribution numbers—again, at least 51% of the funds or equipment or finances used when starting the business should come from this owner. If a 51% LLC has a clause that says something like 80% of the members must agree on something to make a decision or policy, that 51% diverse owner is not in charge on paper—how do you get 80% when 51% and 49% disagree? Note any clause that seems to give the lesser owner permission to make decisions without the diverse owner. Beware if the lesser owners can overrule any decisions or actions the 51% diverse owner(s) wants to make.

Eligibility requirements met: Congratulations, you and your business are certifiable! But, are you sure you want to be?

Who Cares About Certification?

United States Government

The U.S. federal government cares. We remember from the short history of certification in Chapter 1 that Congress set 10% DBE participation goal back in 1983. Well, there have been a few modifications made to that goal. Today the goal is:

- 23% small business (gender & ethnicity neutral)
- 5% small disadvantaged business (minority)
- 5% woman-owned business

- 3% HUBZone small business (SBA program)[12]
- 3% service-disabled veteran-owned business

2019 U.S. Small & Diverse Spending
Totaled $243.9 Billion

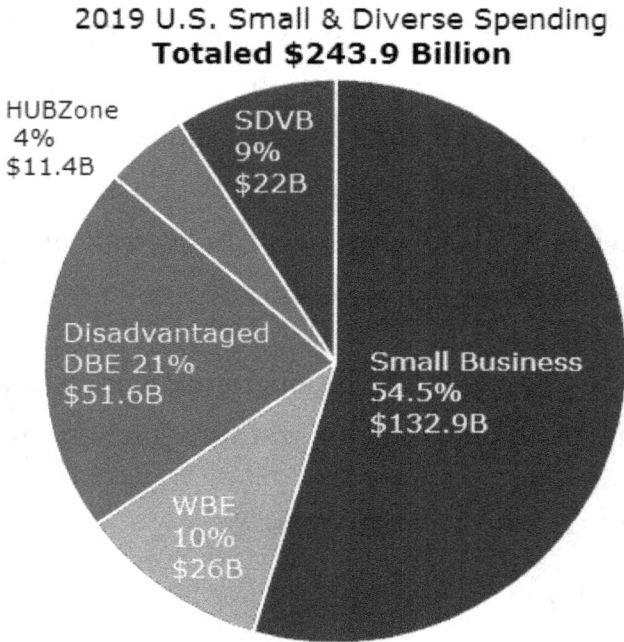

HUBZone
4%
$11.4B

SDVB
9%
$22B

Disadvantaged
DBE 21%
$51.6B

Small Business
54.5%
$132.9B

WBE
10%
$26B

---

[12] This program is based on a business's physical location and requires that 35% of its employees live in a HUBZone. The physical locations depend on census information and are subject to change.

2019 U.S. Subcontracting Goals

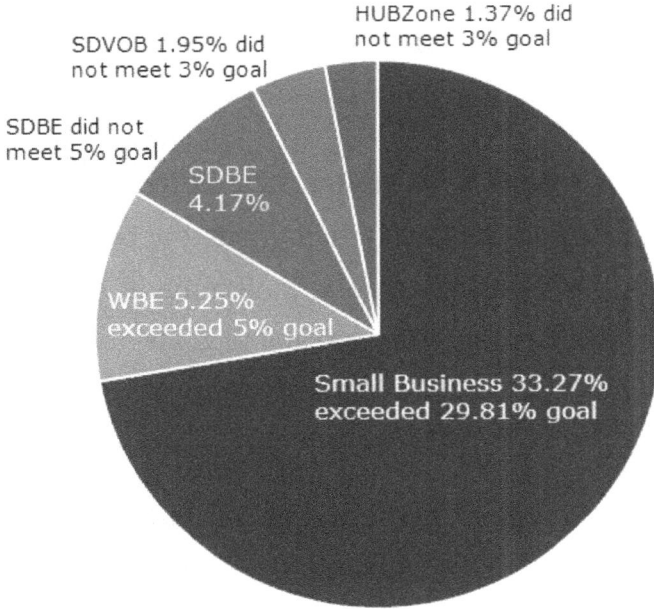

These goals are often mirrored by the corporations who support federal contracts. The U.S. government requires that its big contractors help out by implementing their own contracting programs with diverse spend goals. In 2019, the U.S. government spent $243.9 billion in direct small business contracts, while the big contractors exceeded the subcontracting goals with small businesses—hitting 33.27% spent with small business enterprises (SBEs) and 5.25% with WBEs. They were unable to meet DBE, SDVOB or HUBZone goals. The SBA's 8(a)[13] business development program hit $39.1 billion in 2017 (with an average award of $5.2 million), while the 8(a) contractors reported another $4.6 billion. (SBA Office of Policy, Planning and Liaison, 2020)

Perhaps your business isn't interested in federal government contracting. We were not initially, but on our journey, we discovered that virtually every government agency (state, county, or municipal) has diverse spend goals, too.

Governments Elsewhere

The United Kingdom became the second country to use legislation to address business equity in government purchasing. Its Local Government Act of 2000 "outlined the responsibility that local authorities have to promote the social, economic, and environmental well-being of their communities through diverse procurement practices." (Parliment, 2000) In 2006, France and other EU countries jumped on the bandwagon, promoting "socially responsible public procurement best practices [...] to ensure equality throughout the supply chain." (Korkeoja, Juha, 2016)

---

[13] 8(a) program is a one and done opportunity for a small disadvantaged and/or diverse business to grow their business through government contracting.

In 2014, the European Union published policy encouraging public authorities (government agencies) to engage in responsible procurement "to create job opportunities, decent work, social and professional inclusion and better conditions for disabled and disadvantaged people." But, since these acts and policies are simply aspirations with no tie to specific procurement goals and reporting, these efforts don't seem to have the same impact on diverse suppliers' ability to sell goods and services to government agencies that we enjoy in the United States. (Juncker, Jean-Claude, 2014)

Corporations

And, lest we forget, the world's corporations have their own diverse supplier spend goals. The Billion Dollar Roundtable (BDR), an organization comprised of 28 U.S. corporations with an international footprint, exists to "lead, influence and shape supplier diversity excellence globally." (Billion Dollar Roundtable, 2010) To become a member, companies must:

- Be a viable corporation or for-profit business enterprise which sources minimally $1.0 billion on a first-tier basis to minority- and women-owned business enterprises

Certify and Sell

- Have an established supplier diversity program with the appropriate resources to manage outreach and influence both the internal and external customers [i.e. level 4 or higher as described in Ralph G. Moore and Associates/National Minority Supplier Development Council (RGMA/NMSDC profile[14])
- Be able to audit and verify dollars sourced to minority and women suppliers
- Have any M/WBE, veterans, LBGT, or disabled suppliers certified by NMSDC or WBENC
- Have a 2nd tier program
- Be a member of NMSDC and WBENC[15]

As a member, they actively honor their responsibility by:

- Maintaining $1.0 billion sourcing to minority and women suppliers on a 1st tier basis
- Reporting, auditing, and verifying dollars sourced to minority and women suppliers
- Sharing best practices

---

[14] http://www.rgma.com/rgma-5-levels

[15] https://www.billiondollarroundtable.org/criteria

- Coaching others in the field of supplier diversity
- Striving to increase sourcing to minority and women suppliers each year

The five levels of supplier diversity described by NMSDC and referenced by the BDR are:

- 5 World Class—A company like Level 4 who in addition has savvy, enlightened senior management teams and world-class supplier diversity professionals.
- 4 Advanced—Organizations whose supplier diversity initiative aligns with their strategy, structure, and culture.
- 3 Traditional—The gateway to Advanced and World-Class membership with good processes. However, a lack of alignment between supplier diversity and key initiatives, such as strategic sourcing and marketing, continues to present roadblocks to progress.
- 2 Basic—Companies whose only objective is to satisfy customer requirements or respond to a lawsuit or other organizations that are just passing through.
- 1 Beginning—Organizations that have made a recent decision to embrace supplier diversity and are now examining how supplier diversity can fit into their business model.

- o Zero—Companies and institutions that have no functional supplier diversity program in place and shows no signs that this condition will change.

In recent years, BDR has recognized the U.S. Business Leadership Network (USBLN; now Disability:IN) as the certifier of DOBE (disability owned businesses), the NGLCC (National Gay & Lesbian Chamber of Commerce) as certifier of LGBTBE (lesbian, gay, bisexual, or transgender-owned businesses), NVBDC (National Veteran Business Development Council), and NaVOBA (National Veteran Owned Business Association) as certifiers of veteran businesses.

In 2017, the BDR averaged $2.9 billion per member or about $84 billion; they spent 10.9% of that with diverse suppliers (about $15.9 billion). What about other Fortune 500 companies, 97% of which have supplier diversity programs with varying goals? In 2016, Kenton Clarke at Omnikal.com reported that "$104 billion has been reported by a third-party agency of diverse spend among Fortune 500 companies." Altogether this came to a $509.5 billion pie.

Since multinational companies take a more global view of their supply chains, significant commitment to supplier diversity is beginning to emerge in other countries. We don't have the numbers or percentages to report on those areas at this time, but "as more and more countries embrace supplier diversity, whether, through legislative mandate, social responsibility, economic empowerment, or a combination of all three ..." we can expect the numbers to grow. Because the United States government agencies and corporate entities are experienced with diversity and inclusion, it's easy to imagine these countries might look to our third-party certifiers and reporting structures to adopt similar processes as they structure their own best practices.

By the way, we are talking about the *goals* for diversity spending. ***Being able to sell a diverse business's goods and services does not depend on being certified!*** However, holding a valid certification is the only way for a client to consider the amount they spend with a provider toward its supplier diversity objectives. Because virtually every government agency and many of the world's commercial enterprises have supplier diversity programs, it isn't unusual for many business owners to hear about certification from a big potential customer. We have heard a variety of stories that begin with someone learning about certification at a networking event, a conference, or when they registered in the targeted customer's supplier portal. Others are concerned because a current customer has merged and the new entity wants to know if they're certified. Chasing a big carrot, these owners are rushing to learn about certification, often wanting to know how fast we can make it happen for them.

Because we're certification neutral, we start by asking who the target customer-base is or will be. We believe the business owner should choose certifiers based on what is most advantageous for their own business. If this possible customer has recommended a specific certification, then it seems pretty certain that company will be able to accept or recognize that certification if they buy goods or services from you. But, unless they are already a client, the one thing you don't know is whether being certified will actually help you get business from that client. They might not even know, but they are telling you the odds are better if you're certified.

A Word About IBM

IBM has been in business a very long time. We were privileged to have a guided tour of the museum in Endicott, where the original parquet factory floors glistened and fantastical equipment was displayed. Joanne found herself explaining punch cards and sorters to her teenage daughter Marian as Ed Miller showed us around. We were a direct supplier to IBM at the time, and it is interesting to note that our very first supplier diversity questionnaire came from IBM in 1986.

IBM has been at the forefront of diversity and inclusion as far back as 1899, when it "hired three women, Emma Manske, Nettie Moore and Lilly Philp, 20 years before women were given the right to vote. The same year, IBM hired Richard MacGregor, IBM's first black employee, ten years before the founding of NAACP (National Association for the Advancement of Colored People) and 36 years after the Emancipation Proclamation." And, "IBM hired its first employee with a disability, 59 years before the passage of the Rehabilitation Act of 1973 and 76 years before the Americans with Disabilities Act." (Saylor Academy, 2012)

You'll find IBM in a seat at the Billion Dollar Roundtable and as a sponsor of the third-party non-profit certifiers. IBM was the first founding partner for the National Gay and Lesbian Chamber of Commerce. While no longer a client, we believe IBM deserves recognition for its long-term commitments to diversity and inclusion.

Chapter 3: What's With All That Supporting Documentation?

Often asked in a harried tone, the question we get most often is, "Why am I required to provide all this supporting documentation to get certified?" The simple answer? Fraud.

There are many ways to cheat, most of them complicated and easily discovered. In 2016, The U.S. government recovered $4.7 billion from companies that essentially robbed American taxpayers. The False Claims Act (FCA), known as the "Lincoln Law," is used to impose liability on people or companies (typically federal contractors) who defraud governmental programs. Between 2013 and 2017, 1,059 criminal cases of contracting fraud occurred just in the Department of Defense (DOD) that resulted in 1,087 defendant convictions. Reported cases involved 678 individual persons and 409 businesses. In addition, there were 443 fraud-related civil cases that resulted in judgments against 546 defendants. (Department of Defense, 2018)

Our research introduced us to hundreds of stories, but none more disheartening than this one that resulted in a guilty plea and $50.7 million restitution. Caught by a health-care fraud investigator, Miami psychiatrist Dr. Fernando Mendez-

Villamil pled guilty to healthcare fraud in May 2016, for which he surrendered his medical license and must serve a 12-½ year sentence in federal prison. His false diagnoses caused Social Security to make $20.3 million in undeserved disability payments. The Medicaid program was billed $25.9 million in false claims, including $16.7 million for office visits that never occurred and for medications not needed or taken. False claims under the Medicare program totaled $15.8 million. And false diagnoses to help immigrants bypass portions of the U.S. citizenship test resulted in waivers of more than $814,000 in immigration fees. For just one man with three employees, $62.8 million is certainly fraud on a grand scale. And, oh by the way, he paid his employees under the table, defrauding us all again on payroll and social security taxes. (Richey, Christian Science Monitor, 2017)

The most common fraud schemes include product substitution, false claims or overcharging, falsified quality control testing, embezzlement and theft, bribery and kickbacks, racketeering, prevailing wage avoidance and disadvantaged business enterprise usage. We are including detailed descriptions of different types of fraud to help you identify and avoid unintentionally engaging in practices that could be detrimental to you and your business.

Product Substitution(s): This is when a vendor knowingly substitutes sub-standard, used, or counterfeit products or materials without the consent of the buyer for what was specified by purchase order, contract, or sales agreement. If the buyer is informed and agrees, contracts or agreements can be modified, but failing to deliver and hiding that failure is one form of fraud.

False Claims and Over-Charging: Related primarily to government procurement, if a supplier misrepresents a product in any way, say about its country of origin or the materials used in constructing it, they have made a False Claim. Over-Charging is a pretty simple concept—if the contract allows for a 12% mark up on goods or services, you best not be collecting 12.5%!

Falsified Quality Control Testing: Contracts can have quality standards that you are required to meet. This generally involves some sort of measurement and testing. Reporting false quality results is a form of fraud.

Embezzlement and Theft: Embezzlement is theft ... the embezzler simply steals or misappropriates money or property from someone (employer, partner, person) who trusted them with an asset.

Joanne was in Houston the day the Enron story hit the news, and every single appointment she had scheduled that Friday in August 2001 was cancelled. Its ultimate conclusion led to the Sarbanes Oxley Act (SOX) that established new requirements and standards for financial reporting by U.S. public company boards, management and public accounting firms. Some of the SOX provisions apply to privately held companies including small, diverse businesses, particularly regarding the "willful destruction of evidence to impede a federal investigation." Enron was involved in serious corporate corruption and accounting fraud because deregulation had allowed less government oversight. (Congress, H. R. 3763, 2002)

Ultimately, Enron seriously overstated its earnings reports and created a fake energy crisis, and company executives embezzled retirement funds. The corporation went bankrupt, shareholders lost $74 billion and CEO Jeff Skilling received a 24-year federal prison sentence. The scandal caused its auditors, Arthur Andersen, one of the top accounting firms, to dissolve.

Bribery and Kickbacks: Bribery is traditionally a form of bid-rigging, or getting companies and government agencies to see a company's proposed offerings as most favorable. It has a long and storied history in countries around the world, where baksheesh ("a gratuity, tip, or bribe paid to expedite service"[16]), is almost an expected cost of doing business.

Years of publicized bribery and kickback cases are at the root of many government and corporate "no gift" policies. It is a simple and effective way to avoid any conflicts of interest. The federal government has rules about acceptance of gifts or hospitality published by the Office of Government Ethics. (US Government, 2019) State governments and individual companies have their own policies. We could bring donuts to meetings with a New York state client but could not take the CIO to lunch. One corporate client isn't allowed to accept an advertising pencil. It is best to ask before you put a potential customer in the difficult position of having to refuse your well-meant gift.

Racketeering: In 1970, Congress passed Racketeer Influenced and Corrupt Organizations Act (RICO) as part of the Organized Crime Control Act. It gave federal prosecutors broad powers to charge "alleged organized criminals with committing a series of crimes or what amounts to a pattern of racketeering." In the mid-1980s, about 9% of RICO related to

---

[16] https://www.yourdictionary.com/baksheesh

typical mobster activity, while 81% of all RICO suits filed involved alleged securities fraud, business disputes, or antitrust allegations, according to an American Bar Association study. (Richey, Racketeering Act turns on corporations, 1985)

Prevailing Wage Avoidance: Many contracts include prevailing wage language. Several of our state contracts require us to abide by prevailing wages, though we have not yet been required to report on those wages. The Davis Bacon Act of 1931 established the rule for payment of local prevailing wages on public works projects. If a government contractor submits a certified payroll report with misclassified workers or falsely claims to be paying prevailing wages, it violates the Davis Bacon Act and the False Claims Act (FCA). Workers are able to enforce the right to a prevailing wage by filing legal action under the FCA if they believe an employer is violating Davis Bacon.

Disadvantaged Business Enterprise Usage & Fraud

History of Fraud

Fraud in DBE programs likely began immediately after it was created in 1983. DOT's Office of the Inspector General (OIG) investigated 89 federal allegations of fraud nationally between

1983 and 1988. (Wade, 1982) A detailed review was conducted by the Government Accounting Office (GAO) that resulted in a 58-page report to Senator Daniel P. Moynihan who was then chairman of the Subcommittee on Water Resources, Transportation, and Infrastructure under the Committee on Environment and Public Works of the U.S. Senate in November 1988. They closed 70 of the cases:

- 53 were closed administratively, 21 of which resulted in actions against the contractors
- 17 involved litigation
    - 12 convictions
    - 5 acquittals
- $1,040,434 dollars in restitutions

Another 90 state cases were investigated in New York and Pennsylvania, with 61 cases resolved administratively by taking action against the contractors or closed due to lack of evidence. (Peach, 1988)

Twenty-one years later, the GAO reported a new 2009 case-study of ten firms that received approximately $100 million from service-disabled veteran-owned small business (SDVOSB) contracts through fraud or abuse of the program, or both. It also reported that $187 million was awarded to ineligible HUBZone businesses. And, in 2010, a GAO report noted 14 ineligible 8(a) firms received $325 million from various government agencies. In 2014, the Small Business Administration's Inspector General Report showed that over $400 million in 2013 contracts were awarded to ineligible firms. (Kutz, 2009)

In March 2016, DOT reported spending about $50 billion per year on construction programs, with 10% to DBEs, or $5 billion. Between January 2011 and 2016, DOT OIG's DBE fraud investigations resulted in:

- Over $245 million in financial recoveries, restitution, and forfeitures
- 425 months of incarceration
- 1,161 months of probation and supervised release
- 1,340 hours of community service (Mizer, 2016)

Two years later, in June of 2018, SBA Office of the Inspector General (OIG) "found that Federal agencies' contracting officers and firms did not comply with Federal regulations for 50 of the 56 program sole-source contracts, valued at $52.2 million. *As a result, there was no assurance that these contracts were awarded to firms that were eligible to receive sole-source awards under the Program."* (The emphasis is ours.) (Clark, 2018)

Why are these programs plagued by fraud?

Perhaps because it seems so easy to perpetrate and the benefits can run into generating millions of dollars in revenue for the fraudsters. But, DBE fraud can be subject to civil penalties under the Federal False Claims Act of 1863. This statute was enacted over concerns that some suppliers of goods provided to the Union army during the Civil War were defrauding the government. The law applies to "any person who knowingly submits a false claim to the government or causes another to submit a false claim to the government or knowingly makes a false record or statement to get a false claim paid by the government." Fines can be triple damages with penalties ranging from $5,500 to $11,000 dollars per claim. This per claim fine could have an enormous impact on awarded damages.

The federal government is shutting down its self-certification of women-owned small businesses. In a program that was begun in 2010, NASA's Office of the Inspector General (OIG) reported in 2013 that 35 percent of the WOSBs it contracted with "may not have met the criteria for a woman-owned small business." The self-certification process allows anyone to register their business in SAM (System for Award Management), provide proof of citizenship or permanent residency, minimal documentation on the company structure, and an optional resume. We wrote a blistering blog post in July of that year over our feelings about the people who "falsely self-certify. But there it is ... these companies and people are lying to the federal government. Their lies could well be viewed as theft of taxpayer dollars and theft of opportunity from legitimate WOSBs." (Koprince, SmallGovCon Blog, 2013)

In September 2011, the SBA engaged with a variety of partners to verify WOSB certification applicants (El Paso Hispanic Chamber of Commerce, National Women Business Owners Corporation, U.S. Women's Chamber of Commerce, and Women's Business Enterprise National Council). Oddly, the National Defense Authorization Act of 2015 ended the self-certification program and provided sole source authority. Self-certification continued, and the program was expanded to allow sole-source contracts for WOSBs. Then, in 2018 an SBA OIG review of 2016 and 2017 sole-source WOSB federal contracts "awarded to self-certified women-owned companies showed that 50 out of 56—worth as much as $52 million—did not follow regulations." (Shoraka, 2014) Yet, self-certification did not end until October 2020. (Koprince, SmallGovCon Blog, 2020)

Will it ever end? Probably not. Fraud damages every legitimate diverse business. It is the driving force behind much of the documentation you'll have to provide during the certification process. Personally, we can't fathom the amount of work it takes to support all the lies and scheming, especially when they will get caught. It may take time. As Shakespeare says in *The Merchant of Venice* (2:2): "But in the end **truth will out**."

CUF Not Cuffs

To avoid handcuffs, fines, and jail time, a DBE needs to perform a Commercially Useful Function (CUF). In our industry, we still get calls from primes who want us to use their staff on a project, and we, not so politely, decline. This is termed a pass-through, and though it looks like easy money, the certified company that agrees is putting itself at great financial and legal risk.

Real, substantial penalties can be imposed if we comply with a prime's request to perform as a pass-through subcontractor. Those penalties, beyond financial and potential probation or jail time, also mean the business is likely to be barred from participation in other contracts and will carry the stigma of fraud forever. That's a pretty high price for a few quick bucks.

We believe that this never-ending history of fraud and abuse is the reason certification programs have morphed from a single page verification form into a full-blown certification and supplier diversity industry. The impact of fraud goes far beyond financial. Fraud robs legitimate diverse business owners of opportunities to grow and build their businesses. The insidious nature of pass-through and misrepresentation makes it difficult for diverse business owners to challenge procurement professionals on the value of working with us. And ultimately, fraud in government contracts diverts taxpayer funds to purposes other than those intended—basically ripping us all off.

DBE Fraud Schemes

DBE fraud is often associated with other crimes such as bribery, extortion, money laundering, and tax fraud. These schemes generally fall into two categories:

- Front companies
  - Company exists only on paper
  - Work is performed by the prime or a non-DBE subcontractor

Certify and Sell

- o The DBE is paid a small fee
- Pass Through
  - o The DBE is qualified but doesn't perform a commercially useful function
  - o Some or all of the work is performed by the prime or a non-DBE subcontractor
  - o The DBE is paid a small fee

DBE Fraud Indicators

How to recognize DBE fraud:

- The DBE owner lacks background, expertise or equipment to perform as contractor or subcontractor to complete the assigned tasks.
- The DBE's owner or managers are never present on client site or project and appear not to be supervising its staff.
- Workers shuttle back and forth between prime and DBE payrolls.
- Names on equipment or vehicles are covered with paint or magnetic signs.
- Orders and payments for supplies are made by individuals not associated with the DBE.

- Prime contractor always uses the same DBE. Some DBEs make a practice out of partnering with primes; legitimate DBEs will have the documentation and references to prove the relationship.
- Financial agreements between prime and DBE contractors exist outside normal work, project, or task-based assignments.
- Written contracts or agreements are absent between prime and DBE.
- Prime contractor and DBE have joint bank accounts.
- Prime contractor purchases the DBE-owned business.

Reporting Fraud

If, for any reason, you believe a business is falsely claiming to be certified, please do the right thing. Let the agency they claim to be certified by know. We reported fraud on a Missouri DOT contract in the early 2000s. We'd been engaged by a Virginia-based company to be the WBE subcontractor on a traffic camera system. They named us to win the award and had us do a little bit of work—but nothing that was commercially useful. We never collected what was owed, and Missouri tax payers were defrauded.

Certify and Sell

You can report fraud anonymously with the DOT program through their hotline

- **Call:** 1-800-424-9071 (toll free)
- **Email:** hotline@oig.dot.gov
- **Mail:** DOT Inspector General, 1200 New Jersey Ave SE, West Bldg 7th Floor, Washington, D.C. 20590
- For more information about whistleblower protection, visit https://www.oig.dot.gov/investigations/dot-employee-whistleblower-protection

Other certifiers will have their own procedures.

"Three companies have been selected by the Tribal 8(a) CEO for teaming consideration under your NAICS code(s) from a pool of companies evaluated and recommended by ALBET Enterprises, Inc. (ALBET). Each company successfully completed the ALBET Non-Disclosure & Non-Circumvention (NDNC) Agreement and ALBET Statement of Qualifications (SOQ) process in order to qualify for an ALBET site evaluation. Your company is being granted the opportunity to be the *Primary Teaming Partner* via ALBET."

Extracted from letter to Abator, dated March 3, 2007

Our Other Fraud Experience

If it sounds too good, it is probably a scam ... but in 2007 we were approached by Albet Enterprises, Inc. of Las Vegas. Their strategy was to build teams of subcontractors to assist them in pursuit of federal contracts using their SBA Native American 8(a) status. The pitch involved Albet working with our company and two other designated vendors pursuing federal engagements in custom computer software design and development. Each engagement would have its own teaming agreement specifying which organization would serve as prime and who would be subcontractors. At the time, we were an 8(a) certified disadvantaged Women Business Enterprise holding a master U.S. General Services Administration (GSA) ITS70 (Information Technology Services) contract. It seemed like great way to build a federal practice. We did our due diligence—checked with the Better Business Bureau and the SBA, Googled the company, and had our attorney review the agreements. We decided to move forward based on the letter we received on March 3, 2007.

There we were, the favored *primary teaming partner* with an opportunity of our own. We were keen to bring Albet into our Navy Supply Information Systems Activity (NAVSISA) proposal because it would make our bid stronger. However, during the proposal development, we discovered that what they provided as past performance references weren't theirs but belonged to two other "primary teaming partners" who were also direct competitors of ours on commercial client sites. And, when reviewing their narrative, we discovered that Albet was actually under contract to the Tribe. We made the proposal work and actually won an IDIQ (indefinite delivery, indefinite quantity) contract, but what we had learned led us to file a complaint with the Nevada Attorney General and the Federal Trade Commission. (Copies of our letters are in the Appendix FTC Complaint.)

We learned so much from this experience. With much more historical information now available just a few key strokes away, it is much easier to evaluate potential partner. In 2011, we were surprised by a phone call from South Dakota's Division of Criminal Investigation. Apparently, the Albet principal we dealt with was arrested on two counts of aggravated grand theft by deception, two counts of grand theft by deception, and one count of forgery for misleading "investors to the legitimacy of a tribal charter to open and operate a credit union located on the Yankton Sioux reservation." (Dockendorf, 2011) We certainly learned from this experience and dig much deeper before entering into any new partnership agreements!

Chapter 4: U.S. Certifiers

When we talk about certification, unless otherwise noted we're speaking about programs in the United States. This is the market with which we are most familiar. Certifications are offered by various government agencies at the federal, state, and local level and through third-party certifiers. Technically, some certifications offered through the SBA are actually business development programs. This is especially true of the 8(a) program—officially known as The Minority Small Business and Capital Ownership Development Program.

It was 1970, during the Nixon administration that began the SBA's policy of using Section 8(a) to "assist small concerns owned by disadvantaged persons to become self-sufficient, viable businesses capable of competing effectively in the market place." In 1978, Congress restricted the SBA Section 8(a) to subcontract with "socially and economically disadvantaged small business concerns," or businesses that are at least 51% owned by one or more socially and economically disadvantaged individuals and whose management and daily operations are controlled by such individual(s). Or, the origin of our basic definition for *socially disadvantaged individuals*.

Certify and Sell

The first Department of Transportation (DOT) DBE was passed by Congress as a statutory provision in 1983 to:

- "Ensure nondiscrimination in the award and administration of DOT-assisted contracts;
- Help remove barriers to the participation of DBEs in DOT-assisted contracts, and
- Assist the development of firms that can compete successfully in the marketplace outside of the DBE program."

And, it required that at least 10% of DOT's highway and transit federal financial assistance programs be spent with DBEs. In the 1987 reauthorization, Congress added women to its definition of groups presumed to be disadvantaged.

We have a lot of historical forms, including both a 2002 DOT DBE and 2003 8(a) application. The information and supporting documents required were very similar, as you would expect given the memorandum of understanding between the two federal agencies. Both agencies collect data about the business and its capabilities, owners, and financial and contracting history. Both expect the business owners to be financially disadvantaged and require that owners complete a personal net worth statement, documenting that their total assets not exceed the allowable amount. Historically, the net worth form appears identical between the two agencies. What's not identical is the narrative regarding social disadvantage. DOT doesn't have a specific form for applicants to complete, but rather gathers that information anecdotally during site visits, or through questions it might ask during the file review process.

These programs may require a narrative detailing the issues that make the owner(s) worthy of the social disadvantaged status. If the owner is not a member of a presumed disadvantaged group, which includes African American, Asian American, Hispanic American, and Subcontinent Asian American, then they will be expected to provide "preponderance of evidence" based on discrimination through racial or ethnic prejudice or cultural bias. In our review of DOT appeals, we've seen bias documented based on education, disability, veteran status, and gender bias. The SBA form 1941B also specifically mentions:

- Geographic areas isolated from mainstream American society
- Being a Vietnam-era veteran

- Cultural, ethnic, or social background discrimination "which has caused you unemployment, limited educational opportunities or personal deprivation"
- Low-income status because of apparent discriminatory practices

In all cases, the owner is asked if "access to markets, credit and capital or otherwise inhibited your entry into or advancement in the business world." We wrote a guide for narratives several years ago and have included it in the Appendix Social Disadvantage Narrative.

The major difference between DBE and 8(a) is that the 8(a) is a business development program, not a certification. Because of this distinction, there are some fundamental distinctions to be aware of in the SBA's 8(a) business development program.

- Timeframe: Most certifications are valid for a year after being granted, and that status remains, year after year, as long the business continues to meet the eligibility requirements and submits its renewal paperwork. The 8(a) program is limited to nine years, and yes, you'll be required to provide yearly updates similar to what is provided for certification renewal.

- One & Done Business: Once a business has been granted 8(a) status and graduated from the program, it can **NEVER** participate in the program again. For certifications, if a business has let their certification lapse, it can always reapply and be approved, as long as it continues to meet the certifier's eligibility requirements.

- One & Done Owner: If a person owns a business that has been granted 8(a) status, whether it has graduated from the program or not, they can **NEVER** participate in the program again. If you own multiple companies, only one of them can receive 8(a) status. Neither the owner(s) nor the business can repeat through the 8(a) program. For certifications, if you own multiple companies, each company must be certified individually, but there is no limit to how many of them can get certified. The caveat, each company must meet the eligibility requirements of the certifier.

Third-party certification programs are similar to the government programs. All require that the business is 51% owned and operated by people who meet certain conditions regarding either ethnicity, gender, veteran status, sexual orientation, or disability status. Companies need to provide an annual affidavit reporting changes in ownership, management, or business offerings with explanations of any changes.

What's different? The business does not have to meet the SBA's small business size standards, meaning large businesses meeting the ownership criteria may be third-party certified. And, owners are not restricted to specified personal net worth expectations. Third-party certifiers give successful DBE companies a path to remain certified, continuing to support customers.

Choosing a Certifier

Choosing which certification to pursue should be a strategic decision. If the business exceeds the SBA size standards or the owner's personal net worth is above the maximum currently allowed; third-party certifiers may be the best option as their certifications don't rely on those criteria.

Our first recommendation to anyone interested in a diversity certification is to do a little research. First, talk with the people who actually buy from you now. Ask them direct questions about supplier diversity. Would it be beneficial to them if you were certified? If your goods and services are purchased in an informal manner, your direct buyer might not know the added value that certification might bring to his or her company, so be sure to ask if they have a supplier diversity initiative, department, or purchasing official.

If your current clients have a supplier diversity department, contact them. Ask what certifications they accept, and if it is more than one or two, do they have a preference? Ask if they have a bidder registration process and make sure your business is registered in whatever database or website this client uses to identify potential suppliers. If these contacts have the time and inclination to talk, see what other information they might be able to share about how they acquire what you offer – or if any changes in that acquisition process are planned. Take whatever opportunity they allow to find out how this client buys the goods or services you sell. Ask for their advice, and always remember to thank them for whatever information they provide. For example:

- Is the current product or service purchased under an existing contract? If so, can they tell you who the provider is? Is this provider required to meet any diversity goals? When is the contract expected to expire? Do they expect it to be renewed? If not, how will this purchase be made after the contract expires?

- Does the customer put out a formal request for proposals? If so, how do you get on that list? If not, how can you provide a quote?
- Do they currently buy your offering from a certified vendor?

Second, we suggest exploring your own contacts. Do you know any certified businesses in your industry or local community? Ask these contacts who they are certified by and why they chose a specific certification. Inquire about how the certification has helped them. Find out if they had a plan when they began the path to certification, and if it has worked out the way that they expected. What recommendations might they make to someone just starting the process? Do they recommend speaking with anyone else? If so, stay in touch with these new contacts, and be willing to share your experiences, too. Information exchange is advantageous to us all.

Visit the websites of certifying agencies to learn about their process. Talk with their representatives to see what kind of results their members or certified businesses may have reported to them. Does the certifying agency have a formal tracking program, or is this just anecdotal information? Can they tell you what products or services seem to be reporting the best results? Do they offer any services beyond the certification itself? Do you get a feeling that they are invested in the success of the businesses that they certify? Is there a fee associated with this certification program?

Find the organizations that host events or meetings connecting diverse suppliers with purchasers in your community, and make an effort to attend these sponsored events. Good sources of information about these events would be your municipal, county, or state Offices of Minority and Women Business Development, the closest Small Business Administration Office, local college or university business development programs, and diversity-related Chambers of Commerce. Attending these events will provide perspective as you make your decision about which path to take.

Chapter 5: Navigating NAICS

NAICS (the North American Industry Classification System) codes, pronounced "NAKES," can have a profound impact on diverse business enterprises for several reasons.

NAICS is a shorthand description of a business's goods or services that is used by most of the U.S. certifying agencies. There have been previous versions of this code system (1997, 2002, 2007, 2012), but the most recent version is the 2017[17] codes. Their definitions can be found on the U.S. Census website or NAICS.com. You can enter keywords about your business's goods or services to determine what the associated code might be.

For example, if you own a food truck, you might start with a keyword search for that. That gets zero results. "Restaurant" delivered 25 options, while "food" delivered a whopping 139 results, where we finally found NAICS 722330—Mobile Food Services: "This industry comprises establishments primarily

---

[17] The NAICS codes are updated every five years. The Census website already references the 2022 edition. All references to NAICS codes and information regarding them in this chapter comes from their website.

engaged in preparing and serving meals and snacks for immediate consumption from motorized vehicles or non-motorized carts. The establishment is [...] primarily engaged in providing food services from vehicles, such as hot dog carts and ice cream trucks." (Executive Office of the President OMB, 2017)

Diverse businesses should find all of the NAICS codes that might be related to their goods and services. Order them by the best fit/description of your regular offerings to those less frequently sold. The best fit is likely to be the business's primary NAICS code and is usually reported on the business's taxes, but there may be some really close runners up. For our business we have three top codes:

- 541511 Custom Computer Programming Services—engaged in writing, modifying, testing, and supporting software to meet the needs of a particular customer.
- 541512 Computer Systems Design Services—engaged in planning and designing computer systems that integrate computer hardware, software, and communication technologies.
- 611420 Computer Training—engaged in conducting computer training (except computer repair), such as computer programming, software packages,

computerized business systems, computer electronics technology, computer operations, and local area network management.

It seems clear that these codes overlap, and our other five are subsidiary codes related to delivery of these services.

Most certifiers will want you to be able to prove that your business and its diverse owners are capable of delivering the goods or services associated with your NAICS codes. Sometimes, this can be a subjective area for discussion. Do the owners of a traffic flagging business have to go out and flag cars in a construction zone? It depends on the certifier, but the owner(s) better be well versed in the practice of providing the flagging services, be able to hire and manage flaggers, and own the equipment used by the flaggers, and the business needs to be able to deliver those services in a timely and professional manner.

Customers, especially government agencies or large corporations, are likely to release requests for proposals or invitations to bid by NAICS codes and keywords. If you follow some federal requests for information or sources sought, you may have noticed language like this: "The proposed NAICS for this effort is 541612 (size standard $15M) Human Resources

Consulting Services. *Comments on this NAICS and suggestions for alternative codes must include supporting rationale."* This particular information sought request was for a software system (The Defense Human Resources Activity (DHRA), Office of Equal Employment Opportunity (EEO) Solicitation Number: H98210_EEOTRACK on 21 May 2018). We ended up suggesting a few alternatives. We wrote: *"While Human Resources Consulting makes sense given the subject matter of this notice, we would recommend inclusion of codes for software and system development given the agency's desire for a web-based EEOC Complaint Case Management System. These might include 541611 Records Management; 541511 Software analysis and design services, custom computer; 541512 Computer systems integrator services; 541519 Software installation services, computer; or 518210 Data Processing, Hosting, and Related Services."* This approach will give them a broader base of potential responders with excellent solutions, and make the eventual request for proposal more accessible to our solution.

NAICS is getting a little more fluid. Every edition has changes to, expanded descriptions, or new numbers with new or similar descriptions. When new codes are released, review the NAICS website to reconfirm your existing codes, look for additional applicable codes, or if you have a new product or service, to find the appropriate code.

Requesting a new code from a certifier can be difficult, particularly if the product or service is significantly different from your traditional offerings. **Diverse businesses should request any and all codes they believe applicable with their initial application.** The certifier may ask why a particular NAICS was selected and then determine, based on your explanation, whether to include that code as a part of your certification.

A business's certification letter or certificate lists all NAICS the certifier has approved. Be sure to verify your codes when you get the certificate. We know of an instance when a state agency changed a diverse business's code to 561320 Labor (Except Farm) Contractors (i.e. Personnel Suppliers) when the code requested was 541512 Computer Software Consulting Services or Consultants. Getting it fixed was harder than getting certified in the first place!

Know your codes—you'll never know when they may be requested. And listing your NAICS on your website and capabilities statement can be beneficial to potential customers who are searching for goods or services you offer.

Chapter 6: Other Codes

Codes to describe a business abound. While most certifiers use NAICS, you may find an application that asks for something else. Ones we've encountered often include:

- United Nations Standard Products and Services Code (UNSPC). The UN codes are very precise, and you can look them up at http://www.unspsc.org/search-code. Using the food truck example, none exist for "food truck," two codes for "restaurants," about 180 for "food," and six for "catering." The closest match might be 90101604 Construction or Worksite Catering Services. Our business has over 30 UNSPCs and eight NAICS.

- Product Service Codes (PSC—federal government). On the food truck front, we could not find anything. Even "food" was hard to find, and we know the government has a whole military to feed, right? We finally found a category called 89 Subsistence (Food), but it lists individual product types such as fruits and vegetables, dairy foods, and eggs. There was nothing that we could point to and say a food truck belongs here.

- National Institute of Governmental Purchasing's Commodity/Services Codes (NIGP—used by state and local governments in North America). Using the food truck example, we immediately found 961-19 Food Trucks and Mobile Catering Carts. It was almost too easy! Each organization that uses NIGP should have a link on their website to their NIGP code. Texas, for example, can be found at https://cmblreg.cpa.state.tx.us/commodity_book/Alpha_index_inquiry.cfm.

- Standard Industrial Classification (SIC) System Search might just be the oldest and most limiting of the classifying systems—it was established in 1937. It's rare, but you'll occasionally see them still in use. OSHA, under the U.S. Department of Labor, provides a SIC manual and search option at https://www.osha.gov/pls/imis/sicsearch.html. A search for "food truck" netted no result. We tried "food," "catering," "restaurant," "cook," and "meal." The closest category was 2099 (Food Preparations, Not Elsewhere Classified) which didn't fit upon reading its description, hence the sparse use of the SIC system.

Chapter 7: Preparing the Application

An application package is not always easy to prepare. Many businesses are disappointed when they learn how long and arduous the process can be. Some are intimidated when they look at the application forms online, some by the long list of supporting documents. There are options—you can engage an attorney or hire consulting experts to undertake the effort on your behalf, if you don't want to invest the sweat equity.

No matter what, the business will need to provide certain information, and it does make the process easier if you organize before you begin. Know your NAICS/UN/SIC/PSC Codes. Have your tax ID (Taxpayer Identification Number [TIN] or Federal Employer Identification Number [FEIN]) handy. Get a Data Universal Numbering System (DUNS) Credit Reporting Number (Dun & Bradstreet), which is free; don't pay for it. The certifiers require the business's references from both bank and customers. The bank reference can be the branch manager where you keep your business or personal accounts. Even if the business is new, some sort of professional references will be required, and they should be people who can speak to the business owner's ability to deliver the goods and services that they say the business provides.

Certify and Sell

Get your supporting documents in order[18]. Don't just make copies. Get these critical documents scanned into a PDF so you will have a permanent electronic copy of all your important business materials. Use flash drives, CDs, or cloud storage to store backups at a remote location, such as your safety deposit box, at a family member's home, and/or with your good friend who lives out of town. Or you could choose a third-party backup service. Having backups of these documents geographically spread out from your office is a risk mitigation strategy that would have been beneficial to a friend of ours who survived Hurricane Katrina. Unfortunately, all of his minority business enterprise and much of his historical records were paper and simply melted in the flooding. Not all disasters are major, but anything that destroys your records can be business ending.

Answers to Organize

Preliminary preparation will make your application process much easier. Let's consider the DOT-based certification application. First, make sure the business meets the eligibility requirements:

---

[18] See Appendix Document List

- Business is for-profit (not necessarily profitable yet, but not organized as a non-profit or charitable organization)
- Business is at least 51% owned by a socially and economically disadvantaged individual(s) who also controls it
  - Socially disadvantaged means qualifying individual(s) who are African American, Hispanic, Native American, Asian-Pacific and Subcontinent Asian American, or women. Other individuals may also qualify as socially disadvantaged on a case-by-case basis.
  - Economically disadvantaged means qualifying individual(s) personal net worth does not exceed $1.32 million, excluding the value of the business being certified, the value of the owner's primary residence, and in most circumstances, the value of the owner's retirement account
- Disadvantaged owners are U.S. citizens or lawfully admitted permanent residents of the United States.

- Business meets the Small Business Administration's size standards and does not exceed $23.98 million in gross annual receipts[19].

Make a list of the business owners, note their title, gender, and ethnicity and how much of the business they own or control. Find out how long they have had ownership and how they became owners (started, bought, inherited, etc.). Gather their home addresses, phone numbers, and what resource amounts, cash or otherwise, they may have used to acquire their ownership position. Expanding on this list, document the frequency (always, often, seldom, or never) each:

- Sets policy for company direction/scope of operations
- Handles bidding and estimating
- Makes a major purchase
- Is responsible for marketing and sales
- Supervises field operations (if your company has field operations)
- Performs office management
- Hires and fires management staff
- Hires and fires field staff

---

[19] This threshold is periodically adjusted for inflation.

- Decides what to do with profits and investments
- Obligates the business by contract or credit
- Purchases equipment
- Signs business checks

Make a list of the equipment and vehicles that the business uses to produce its goods and services, noting whether each is owned or leased. Gather the company's banking information, including the bank official responsible for the account. Make a list of the three largest projects (or sales) competed in the last three years, including a contact with phone number and email, brief description of goods or services sold, address of client/work and the dollar value of the work done. Do the same with your three largest current projects. Pull together the list of required documents in the Appendix DOT Unified Certification Supporting Documents.

What about Missing Documents?

People and businesses can misplace paperwork. We've moved seven times in 37 years, which has provided ample opportunities for us to lose paper-based records and led us to our recommendation that business owner's scan their important documents and store electronic copies in multiple locations. Virtually every certifier will ask owners to prove their initial contribution in establishing a business. The first time we were asked to provide this financial proof was 2002, about 19 years later. We had documented those contributions in the general ledger and in the minutes of the corporation, but not even the federal government expects us to keep financial records beyond seven years. We wrote a legal statement about the contributions of the owners and had it notarized, which ended up being sufficient. However, it would be best to check with the certifier and find out what they are willing to accept in place of a missing document.

Missing material can be approached in different ways. For initial investments: the bank may be able to provide a copy of the initial deposit used to open the business account, perhaps the originating bank has a cancelled check for that deposit, the attorney could offer a copy of the original invoice for organizing documents, or the state's Secretary of State might offer a receipt for the funds spent to register the business.

Disadvantaged Narratives ... the SBA 8(a) Program

What is disadvantaged? There is no single answer, but a simple description might be "a systematic or systemic barrier to opportunity." To become SBA 8(a) program certified, the business owner must write a narrative describing the disadvantages or discrimination experienced. It can be intimidating to revisit and write about victimization. And, in this narrative, you must write about your personal experience and how these incidents have had a negative impact on your ability to achieve expected outcomes. This can include educational-, financial-, racial-, gender-, geographical-, and employment-related events throughout your life. And, you may be able to use publicly available demographic or statistical information to establish a pattern of discrimination in your field of expertise.

When writing your narrative, the first step is a generic statement: "I perceive I have experienced professional rejection for reasons of" followed by the reasons like ethnic origin, disability, residence, gender, race, education. Then, you will need to write about specific instances of bias against you and how this bias has had a negative impact on your ability to enter into or advance in business. The narrative writing exercise can be made easier by breaking it down into manageable topics such as access to education or capital, discrimination in the work place, educational institution, lenders, physical ability challenges, or societal expectations.

Physical challenges, or having a disability, may be the easiest to address, not because the challenge of overcoming physical limitations is easy but because these challenges are often visible and fairly easy to document. Physically speaking, those of us who are handicapped face bias because we're taken less seriously than those who appear whole. For example, Joanne is never without her crutches. You'll observe she's at the back of the pack in any walking excursion. She can't golf, not just because she can't keep up with the caddie, but because structurally she can only hit the ball with a wicked left spin. So, when it comes to the proverbial deal on the golf course (or tennis/basketball courts) she can't physically participate. And, her physicians are happy to document the problem, hence her handicapped parking placard. None of her certifications (until 2017) are based on her physical disabilities, but this is an example of how one might approach limitations on potential opportunities due to physical challenges.

As for education, think about these issues and whether systemic bias interfered with you regarding:

- Admissions criteria for college or advanced training
- Membership in school clubs, fraternities, or professional organizations
- Educational honors or recognition
- Scholarships or financial support
- Harassment in the education institutions

- Social pressures that discouraged you from seeking higher education or training
- Access to mentoring, on-the-job training, apprenticeships

Gender discrimination in schools is usually based on cultural assumptions that males and females are skilled in different areas of academics, for example home economics vs. shop. Racial discrimination in education is generally based on similar cultural assumptions about which group traditionally excels at a particular skill. Pennsylvania provides detailed definitions of illegal discrimination in its educational institutions. They include classmate harassment or bullying, teacher requests for sexual favors in return for grades or repeated sexual comments to the student, or classmates repeatedly making sexual comments.

Once you have identified a particular pattern in your educational experience, you'll have to write about how those experiences affected you in business. Being discouraged by family on pursuing a four-year degree was a hindrance to Joanne when she tried for a corporate job in human resources—no college degree, no second interview.

Another area to think about is your employment history. For example, could there have been cultural bias if you experienced:

- Significant variation in compensation and/or fringe benefits from those of equally qualified contemporaries
- Denial of increases, bonuses, or commissions for reasons that were different than those required of other individuals of equivalent qualifications
- Termination for reasons that were different than those applied to other individuals of equivalent qualifications

You can learn more about basic employee rights at the U.S. Department of Labor websites. The 1964 Civil Rights legislation made discrimination illegal. When an employee is not being dealt with the same as his or her coworkers it could be workplace discrimination owing to age, disability, race, religion, gender, etc. The U.S. Equal Employment Opportunity Commission has many reports and articles about workplace discrimination. (Congress, 1964)

Another thing to consider is "access to capital"—a ubiquitous phrase encountered at virtually every small business seminar or networking session. What it boils down to is whether the entrepreneur can get the money they need to start, run, or expand the business enterprise. Historically, small business financing has been problematic. The U.S. Commerce Minority Business Development agency indicates that access to capital is as much an issue today as it was in 1969. They examined "both national and regional studies over several decades and found that limited financial, human, and social capital as well as *racial discrimination* were primarily responsible for the disparities between non-minority and minority businesses."

Dr. Fairlie testified before the U.S. Senate about difficulties minority entrepreneurs face in obtaining financing. The National Association of Women Business Owners (NAWBO) reports that, "Women business owners still face greater obstacles in obtaining financing for their businesses than similarly situated men do. In addition, access to capital by women business owners is not commensurate with their business growth." Your narrative should detail any bias you've encountered in seeking financing.

What about statistics or demographics? The U.S. Census Bureau has a number of business and industry reports and general demographic information that may be helpful in preparing a narrative. For example, the MWBE owner of a Wyoming-based business discovers that the state's population is 90.7% non-minority, and of the 61,179 businesses in the state only 15,608 are women-owned . . . and only 323 of these are minority women-owned. It might be possible to cite this disparity in MWBE ownership as a barrier encountered when developing a new MWBE business in Worland, Wyo.

When writing her narrative in 1994, Joanne discovered that "women represent less than 25% of all computer programmers or software engineers and only 21.7% of chief executives." Fast forward to 2007, and we discover that women own less than 5% of information technology firms. Culturally, it would seem that a WBE-owned IT firm might have bigger hurdles to overcome than its masculine counterparts.

Each narrative is unique, distinct to the individual's life and business experiences. Ask yourself: What's my story?

The Site Visit

We've been visited many times—in person and by phone. And in 2015, we wrote a blog article that we still share with nervous diverse business owners. It used to be that Small Disadvantaged Minority, Women, Veteran, or LQBT-Owned Businesses (SDMWVLGBTs) were certified on faith that owners provided truthful information on application forms and that they really, actually owned and operated their own businesses. Unfortunately, due to the fraud in the early days of certification previously discussed, the certification process itself has become more stringent, and site visits are now the norm. This way, it is well documented that the business owner is, in fact, eligible for certification. Regrettably, it also means that business owners often wonder what's going to happen at the site visit. So, based on our 25+ certifications that came with site visits, this is our list of what to expect:

- Have your photo ID handy, to prove you are you!

The visitor will probably note or ask:

- Is the firm home-based or in an office? If in an office, is your business name publicly displayed (sign on building, door etc.)?
- Do you share space with any other firms? If so, with who? What is the primary business of all firms sharing this space? Are you doing business with any of the firms sharing the space?

Like conversational essay questions, you'll likely be asked to talk about the history and ownership of your business:

- What are the business's primary goods and services (matching your NAICS or other codes)?
- How long have you been in business?

- How did you get involved in the business?
- When did you get involved in the business?
- Why did you start/buy your own business?
- What is your ownership percentage?
- When did you take majority control?
- How did you become qualified to run the business?
- When you started up, what financial or other resources did you contribute? Did others make contributions?
- Who are the other owners, and what percent do they own/vote?
- Why do you want to certify?

And you will probably be asked to talk about current business issues:

- Do the owners owe the business money or vice versa?
- What are the typical daily operations of your business?
- What are your duties and responsibilities as owner?
- How are decisions made if you're not around?
- Who makes final decisions, especially related to governance, control, and financial issues?
- How do you acquire new business?
- Who are your top three customers?

- How much time do you work in/on your business? Or what kind of schedule do you keep?
- Do you work for, own, or manage another business?
- How many employees do you have? What type of hiring/firing processes do you have?
- Is the primary owner the most highly paid? If not, why?
- What plans do you have for your business's future?

Your site visitor will likely want to tour your business facility. The visitor is likely interested to know:

- Is the facility of the sort that can deliver your business's goods or services?
- Are you knowledgeable about the facility and any major equipment/department areas?

See, not so tough after all!

Chapter 8: Not Guaranteed Certification

Not every legitimate diversely owned business gets certified the first time around. No one involved in the certification process wants to allow a fraudulent application to be approved. In the early days of the program, when self-certification was the norm, fraud usually involved setting up a—or finding an existing—company headed by a diverse leader. The non-minority contractors would do the paperwork to win the projects, supply the staff, do the work, and give the diverse company a percentage of the profits. Most of the onerous certification and contract monitoring processes grew out of those dishonest practices. We wrote in Chapter 2 about governance and control—areas that analysts may find errors in paperwork or issues in actual performance and, the sometimes-subjective nature of an application's review.

Real Reasons for Denial

Caveat: *Almost all of the certifiers will help you for free when you are completing their application form. They will explain their forms and tell you what supporting documents you need.* But, beware! Staff members and volunteers are generally not allowed to discuss the contents of your application with you before it is formally submitted. They can't give you a heads up if you have intrinsic errors or issues that will result in a denial. Government agency employees are subject to laws, while third-party suppliers have their own rules and regulations. It is always a good idea to have your attorney or a neutral expert review your file for completeness and compliance with the certification rules.

There are very real reasons for an application to be denied. Certifiers will provide a denial letter to the business owner(s) which explicitly details why they were not certified. To better understand denials, we've summarized a few cases:

A woman who had previously been certified 100% women-owned LLC brought in a new 49% male partner. Unbeknownst to her, the attorney used boiler plate language that impacted her ability to govern and control her business. She trusted the attorney, executed the operating agreement, and was stunned when her company became decertified. She believed it was a political issue until we were requested to review her application. The new operating agreement contained language about unanimous and/or a required 80% agreement between the members to break a tie on a contested issue. It also gave her new partner first right of refusal if she wanted to dispose of her ownership; she expected her son to eventually receive her shares but the new agreement interfered with that plan. Because of the 80% rule, she couldn't unilaterally do anything, including buying out the new partner. The lesson in this case is, make sure your attorney understands the rules for certification and insist that they explain the ramifications of changes in plain English—and, don't sign anything until you are absolutely sure you understand them.

A new LLC was 51% minority women-owned, with a 49% Caucasian male partner. They sought the advice of their local certifying agency in preparing the application and ended up denied for several reasons. The attorney had advised each owner to contribute the same amount of cash and used boiler plate language in the operating agreement. Again, the boiler plate included terminology about unanimity, and in this case neglected to identify the 51% owner as the managing member. There were other errors in her application, mostly on the resume and description of who was responsible for certain tasks. Oddly, the certifier allowed both members to be in the site visit interview. Technically, only the minority woman should have been interviewed. Like many of us, this owner has a tendency to say "we" instead of "I" in an effort to be more inclusive. During the application process and site visit, the diverse owner must remember that they are the one in charge of the business and that the buck stops with them; otherwise, it is possible for the certifier's analysts to assume the non-diverse owner has too much power to control or govern the business.

Many years ago, as a volunteer site visitor for a certifier, Joanne called on a company that had recently become 100% women-owned. The business was in construction and the state had denied her certification because she didn't physically go out on the flagging crews, even though she supervised them. When asked why she decided to take over the entire company from other family members she burst into tears, stating she didn't understand why people kept asking her that question. Joanne asked because as CEO of a family-owned company she was genuinely curious. This woman had always been 51% owner and had bought out her husband and son. It turns out that was why the state denied her—they made an assumption that the recent stock exchange was an attempt to create a front, with the guys pulling strings behind the scenes. The certification analyst completely missed her 51% ownership from the very start of the business. The third-party certifier was poised to deny as well, until the site visit cleared up the issue. The lesson learned here is, if ownership has recently changed, be prepared to be scrutinized.

Certify and Sell

In a similar, but inside out visit, the 51% minority women-owned and operated business was denied by the third-party certifier. The business owner insisted that she had 51% interest, but the documents she showed clearly stated that the partners would share equally in the risks and profits of their business. It can't be equal, unless the business is 50/50 owned by women or 50/50 owned by members of an ethnic minority. The state, however, certified her and her business.

Sometimes rules change. Trusts are a complicated issue and something to have clarity on before applying for certification. We have some shares held in trust for Joanne's grandchildren, stock that is controlled and voted by their aunt who is our CFO, which is pretty clear and doesn't impact our primary owner's 71% position anyway. But there are times, particularly in family-owned businesses that involve parents and grandparents who may have been the founding members of a company, where ownership in the company may be held in trust. There are two types of trusts, revocable and irrevocable. Revocable means the person(s) who established the trust can take it back—whether it is stock or cash, it still belongs to the person(s), aka grantor, who granted the trust. An irrevocable trust, one that can't be undone, may be made by any person(s) and managed by either a diverse trustee or a financial institution on behalf of a diverse beneficiary.

The point of this story is a rule change. One owner was denied third-party certification because the trust was not managed by a diverse trustee. Today, the rule has been changed because a beneficiary of a trust can't be expected to dictate who manages the trust, especially in the case where a financial institution is responsible. Imagine if Joanne put the grandchildren's stock in a trust managed by a major bank, then tried to dictate that only female bank employees could serve as trustees. Somehow, we don't think that would fly.

Franchise owners may have difficulty obtaining a diverse certification because it is generally assumed that franchisees have little control over the business. If there are standard industry practices, such as in the automotive or chain restaurants, opportunities for certification may exist. Certifiers review franchise agreements very carefully to make sure that the franchisee has a measure of control of his or her business and that the agreement is industry standard.

Subjective Reasons for Denial

Subjective denials occur for what seems like no rational reason at all. We were denied WBE certification from one state agency on the West Coast in the early 2000s because the analyst believed that a male officer who had loaned money to the company could then exercise undue influence on the women who held 87% of the stock. To be fair, the male in question was father to two of the women, but we are organized one share, one vote and both female officers had loans to the company as well. To us, it made perfect sense. The company was willing to pay us the same interest rate as the banks were charging— much more than a savings or certificate of deposit would pay. This agency didn't do a site visit, not even by phone, or they would have discovered that Joanne and her sister had never been particularly controllable.

One DMWBE (disadvantaged minority women business enterprise) had the unique pleasure of being both certified and denied certification at the same time. Subjectively the certifier determined that her business didn't qualify to haul general freight in NAICS codes 414110, 121 or 122, but approved her to haul specialized freight in NAICS 484220. They also suggested a new NAICS 541614 for "Process, Physical Distribution, and Logistics Consulting Services." Her company holds the DOT authority for general freight hauling, and she has negotiated contracts with two owner operators, neither of whom possesses such authority to fulfill the general haulage work orders while a company owned vehicle is in for repairs. Apparently, a truck being operational at the time of the site visit was a critical issue—which was not mentioned when the interview was arranged.

Another family-owned business, 51% women, was denied when the certifier subjectively determined that she wasn't qualified to run a landscaping business. How they managed to overlook her fifteen years of running a similar business, all of its financing, sales, and scheduling functions before starting her new business in 2014 is a mystery. She also made her contribution to starting the business by selling some personal stock that was in her name only, but because she deposited the funds into a joint account to be able to write checks to the attorney and pay required state fees to get the paperwork necessary to establish a business checking account, the analysts determined that these were joint funds. In further discussion, we learned that this joint account was originally her account established while in high school and she added her husband to it after the wedding. It might be better to get cashiers' checks or establish a separate savings account if you find yourself in a similar situation.

In another instance, while not denied by a New England state that required 30 plus years' worth of meeting minutes, it was strongly suggested that we withdraw our application. Of course, we did so. A death had occurred in the family between the submission of our application and the analyst's review. This led the analyst to question control because he didn't believe our corporate bylaws sufficiently defined a quorum, aka the minimum number of voters, needed to pass a resolution. That makes us pretty sure he never read any of the shareholder meeting minutes! Perhaps the language in the original bylaws was confusing, as it says "At any meeting the presence in person or by proxy of shareholders entitled to cast at least a majority of the votes which all the shareholders are entitled to cast in the particular matter shall be necessary and sufficient to constitute a quorum for the purpose of considering such matter." Subjectively, he didn't connect the fact that a single diverse person owns 71% of our shares. She can have a meeting and make decisions by herself any time she so chooses. If for some reason she is incapacitated, our female CFO and 11% owner could certainly have a blast voting another 89% of the shares (the grandchildren and Joanne's).

Sometimes, the sheer amount and complexity of an application's paperwork can muddle the big picture. Particularly, one instance when the owner might have been involved in closing one business while starting a new one and purchasing assets from still others. Three times, a state agency asked one client of ours to amend her personal net worth statement to reflect ownership in another company. There was a real problem with this request. The personal net worth statement was completed in the summer of 2018, and she had sold all of her business interests the previous October. She had no reason to amend the statement. In fact, doing so would have been misrepresentation. In other clarifications, the agency asked for tax returns of the previously sold company and a trust that was based on the stock of that company, which were duly provided. But, then, the agency asked for more detail on the distribution of dividends reported on the trust. Somehow, the agency misunderstood—the trust earned dividends that reduced its net loss for the year. No dividends were disbursed to her. She received a denial determination ("DBE Certification Denial—Failure to Comply") due to these misunderstandings and misinterpretations. After a protest, the agency requested a few documents and scheduled the site visit. Ultimately, this company was denied for control and governance issues that were not related to the requested documents.

In another case, the DOT wiped away one woman's career by misinterpreting a single interview answer. In their denial letter, they said she "indicated that she is responsible for the front office management of the firm and has introduced safety protocols and other standard administrative procedures resulting in the reduction of overtime and unnecessary business expenses." The original evaluation ignores that she had run production jobs in the family's lathe and mill business. They overlooked her experience with a global manufacturer in the same industry but on a much larger scale that became directly beneficial and relevant to her when taking over ownership of the family business. The denial letter minimized her role and prejudicially devalued her contributions while glorifying the contributions of the white male minority owner despite clear evidence that shows she absolutely controls the management, policy, and operations of the business. In just four years of running the business, she raised sales from $500K to over $2 million and implemented new technologies. No wonder the family—who had asked her to run the company—turned the loan she used to acquire her stock into a gift! In the spring of 2020, her appeal was upheld, and the local certifier has issued her certificate.

Potential Fixes

A legitimate diversely owned business has options when denied certification. Yes, harping on legitimacy is part of our shtick. We have absolutely no interest in seeing these certification programs abused or defrauded. So, if a business is faking its diverse status, there is no fix for you. When certification is denied for a real reason, the best option is to fix the issues and reapply when the certifier is willing to accept a new application. The denial letter will be explicit, stating the reason(s) for denial. If you believe the denial was made erroneously, the business can protest within the timeframe allowed by the certifier. In this instance, you will likely want to have your attorney draft a formal letter explaining why the certifier may have misinterpreted the application or documents.

The split decision trucking company mentioned earlier in this chapter is filing an appeal for the denied NAICS codes. They believe that the certifier cherry-picked parts of the contracts between her and her subcontractors, even though she uses industry standard language. DOT agencies—roads, airports, and public transportation agencies—only recognize DOT certifications. Because this business owner holds a third-party certification in those NAICS codes, her ability to be recognized as a WBE by commercial customers is not impacted. The approved NAICS codes allow her to be recognized for her current DOT-related work with specialty trucking.

The woman-owned landscaping business is collecting the documentation to show that the joint account was originally hers and bills of sale to prove that the securities sold were in her name only. She's also revised her resume to highlight the 20 plus years of business management experience the certifier overlooked. And, she's written a history of how and why she decided to start her business in the first place. She will reapply for certification soon.

As for the West Coast agency, a couple of years later, we reapplied and received certification with no issue. In the New England case, we agreed to withdraw and resubmit our application, with amended bylaws, and we were duly certified.

Ultimately, organizing properly in the first place is the best practice toward successfully certifying your business.

Chapter 9: Real World Denials and Appeal Results

We discovered that the DOT posts DBE application denial and appeal information on its website at https://www.transportation.gov/civil-rights/disadvantaged-business-enterprise/denials-appeals. As certification is denied, we were very interested to read up on cases that involved reversals, because many of the denials we'd experienced didn't make sense, especially when ownership changed hands through gifting. Each DBE owner is asked to answer a question about how they acquired the business have five options: Started business myself; It was a gift from (blank); I bought it from (blank); I inherited it from (blank); or Other (blank).

Because it's government, there are layers of laws, acts, and rules that apply to anything done in the name of the United States. The DOT DBE rules get changed through the Supplemental Notice of Proposed Rulemaking (SNPRM) process. And when it comes to gifts, what we found published in June of 2013 reads: "For this reason, the SNPRM erected a presumption that assets acquired by gift in this situation would not count. The applicant could overcome this presumption only by showing, through clear and convincing evidence—a high standard of proof—that the transfer was not for the purpose of gaining DBE certification and that the disadvantaged owner really controls the company." Essentially, this helps protect against fraud without assuming that every gift is simply to gain an illegitimate certification. The same rule goes on to define that it doesn't matter where money comes from once you have invested it in your company.

If loans are involved, extra care must be taken. Official loan documents should detail the value of the loan and terms for repayment. If there is a possibility of loan forgiveness, it should be noted and explained in the loan agreement. Many things could be listed as potential for retiring a loan, such as sales increase of x percent, reduction of overhead expenses by x percent, landing a particular client or contract, or any other legitimate reason that can demonstrate a real, substantial and valid rationale for retiring the loan. No matter what certification an owner might be interested in pursuing, they have all been designed to prevent fraud. If not well documented, gifts or loan forgiveness may be interpreted by a certifier's analyst as being superficial and a front for a non-diverse business to take advantage of a certification to which it is not entitled.

All of our owners were gifted some stock at one point or another. Ultimately, the reason had much more to do with taxes than certification. Family-owned companies pay all sorts of taxes, including inheritance taxes on our private stock. Did it make sense for Joanne's dad to gift his daughters and grandchildren with some of his stock when he turned 70? Of course, it did! But he was no longer actively involved in the business founded by a daughter who was always the majority owner. Other gifts haven't presented quite so cleanly. For the woman whose expertise was ignored, this clause is at the root of her appeal. DOT says all assets are created equal. Given how she has quadrupled revenues by applying her expertise and knowledge, we hope the local certifier's decision will be reversed.

On determining ownership, it is basically agreed that the *"general burden of proof on applicants should be the preponderance of the evidence."* During the same 2013 SNPRM, for situations where a firm was formerly owned by a non-disadvantaged individual, the SNPRM "proposed the higher "clear and convincing evidence" standard, because of the heightened opportunities for abuse involved. The Department believes this safeguard is necessary, and we will retain the higher standard in these situations."

A New Jersey-based logistics company certified in its home state plus at least Pennsylvania, New York, California, and

Virginia applied for interstate certification as a DBE in Colorado in 2015. After CDOT requested substantial information from the owner, "CDOT made over sixteen (16) supplemental requests for additional information and documentation from August 2015 through February of 2016." On appeal, the appeals board found that "CDOT improperly sought information beyond that which an interstate applicant must produce" because the information didn't relate to control of the firm by the disadvantaged owner. Our interpretation is that, if your home state certified you as a DBE, another state's DOT DBE program isn't supposed to conduct a full certification analysis.

The DOT DBE program should be consistent from state to state, and if the home state determines that ownership criteria is met, it isn't subject to another interpretation until or unless the actual ownership changes. When you are a DBE certified company, it is incumbent upon the owner(s) to report any material change within 30 days, especially if such change impacts certification criteria. DBE ownership may not fall below 51%.

Too close or intertwined for comfort, an Arizona business was originally denied because, while the DBE owner met the criteria, his business did not meet the independence test. The rule states: "Only an independent business may be certified as a DBE. An independent business is one the viability of which does not depend on its relationship with another firm or firms." The DOT certifier will review:

- Business relationships with other companies involving personnel, facilities, equipment, financial and/or bonding support, and other resources
- Current or prior employer/employee relationships between DBE owner(s) and those other, non-DBE companies and/or their owners
- The relationship with a prime to determine if pattern of exclusivity with the prime may compromise the DBE's independence
- The relationships between the DBE and other firms to determine if it is typically within normal industry practice

Subsequently, the appeals board determined that while the owner met criteria of 50.1% ownership and was both socially and economically disadvantaged, three other owners (16.3% each) did not. This company under consideration for certification specializes in construction management, contracting, and consulting. And, the other owners have companies in construction, engineering and electric contracting in the same vicinity. In fact, this company rents space from, shares board members, receives free accounting and payroll services, and allows the other companies' owners to sign checks and make hiring and firing decisions. The appeals board determined that this applicant was not independently owned and operated.

As a DBE owner, you must be able to answer this question: if you are faced with the loss of a non-DBE owner or key person, will you be able to hire a replacement to fulfill the primary tasks of that person? The code says: "The socially and economically disadvantaged owners must have an *overall understanding of, and managerial and technical competence and experience* directly related to, the type of business in which the firm is engaged and the firm's operations. *The socially and economically disadvantaged owners are* **not** *required to have experience or expertise in every critical area of the firm's operations, or to have greater experience or expertise in a given field than managers or key employees.* The socially and economically disadvantaged owners must have the ability to intelligently and critically evaluate information presented by other participants in the firm's activities and to use this information to *make independent decisions* concerning the firm's daily operations, management, and policymaking. Generally, expertise limited to office management, administration, or bookkeeping functions unrelated to the principal business activities of the firm is insufficient to demonstrate control."

Chapter 10: Patience with Certifiers

To us, the certifying organizations are made up of the analysts and certifier staff members with whom we have contact. As entrepreneurs we often get to make up our own organizational policies, processes, and procedures as and when we wish ... and then, the people who work in our businesses have to follow them. Sometimes, because we are used to having so much control, we forget that others simply don't. Patience is a key skill we've learned to practice when seeking diversity certification. This is a complicated process with mandated compliance requirements. The mandates may differ slightly between certifiers, but the similarities far outweigh those differences.

Another major similarity is that certifiers are not-for-profit organizations. Unlike us business owners, who must be organized as for-profit for virtually every diversity certification, certifiers are either government agencies or nonprofits. And, most of these certifiers are backlogged with hundreds of pending applications and annual updates. We know the effort that goes into preparing just one application, our own business is certified by 26 states, two cities, and two non-profit agencies and has helped many companies on their own paths to certification. The actual application is eight or nine pages of questions about the owner, the business, its history including references, banking relationships, employees, equipment, etc. If a DBE certification is being sought, three more pages of personal net worth data must be collected. Finally, a stack of supporting documents and an affidavit complete the application. Conservatively, that's likely to be about 200 pages for the certification analyst to review. For a 36-year-old company like ours, it's about a ream of paper (500 pages).

As time-consuming as the process is for us, the information we're providing isn't new. We know our business. The certification analyst doesn't. They start at the equivalent of page one with the name of the business and reads the entire application, cross-referencing with the documents to ensure that the business is truly owned, controlled, and governed by its SDMWVLGBT owner(s). During this review, the analyst may have a question or two. We're notified of the question and given a specific period of time to respond. And, the certifier expects that SDMWVLGBT owner(s) will comply, if not cheerfully at least politely.

Once all the questions have been answered and the documents accounted for and reviewed, the site visit will be scheduled. If the certification sought is DBE through a state government—Department of Transportation (DOT) or Unified Certification Program (UCP), etc.—the visit will likely be conducted by a government employee. And, they likely have a backlog of applications and visits. If it is a third-party certification, volunteers may be involved, serving on committees or other steps in the process, possibly even the site visit. No matter which certifier is chosen, several months may pass between the time an application is submitted and the initial site visit.

As entrepreneurs, most of us are accustomed to demanding clients who expect immediate results, and we jump through hoops to deliver quick, efficient, and effective goods or services. It is easy for us to become frustrated with the certification process. Some become so frustrated that they don't finish the application. Many are overwhelmed by the number of historical documents requested. Others feel the need for personal financial information is too intrusive or view the time commitment as excessive.

It seems natural to us that we expect the certifiers to jump through hoops in evaluating and approving our applications. But, in the real world, these nonprofit or government certifiers are also overwhelmed. As supplier diversity has become a driving force in corporate and government procurement, more businesses apply for certification, and the certifiers, too, become backlogged by the inundation of applications and hundreds of documents to review. Certifiers are faced with incomplete applications, missing materials, or questions about language in governing documents, all of which require extensive communications to resolve before they can schedule the site visit. And don't forget these certifiers also have to review annual affidavits from previously certified companies. Also, site visit scheduling complicates and delays the process. So, it's really no wonder that the wheels of certification seem to grind very slowly. Be patient. It will be worth the wait if you use it right.

Chapter 11: Certified ~ Not a Magic Ticket

Congratulations, you're certified!

Simply being certified isn't going to provide immediate entry into a world of major contracts with huge companies or government agencies. Work still must be done. We chased Mellon Bank for nine years before we did any work with them, and that didn't involve supplier diversity or procurement or even an MSP[20]. It was an era when we were still able to pick up a phone and, on a cold call, speak with a decision maker in the IT department of a large company. We eventually wore them down. They decided to take the leap when they experienced a technical pain, which we were able to address. Ultimately, it turned into a multi-year engagement updating a portfolio of trust accounting software programs. Nine years! They didn't care that we were a certified business because in the early 1990s that wasn't a thing. Today, so many barriers lie between us and our B2B target customers, given interactive voice response systems, email, and social media platforms.

---

[20] MSP – Master Service Provider, aka Gatekeeper who is the funnel for all IT Services

Procurement, too, has changed. It's become a much more formal and often layered supply chain process that can be difficult for smaller businesses to traverse from the black hole of supplier portals to an actual relationship that may lead to a sale.

Certification is a sales and marketing tool. Government agencies and commercial clients are struggling to be more inclusive with their purchasing dollars. When CVM Solutions surveyed 162 supplier diversity professionals in 2018, they discovered that the top three drivers of programs were social responsibility, corporate culture and workplace diversity and inclusion (D&I), and customer requirements. To us, the most telling is customer requirements, because we so often write about walking the walk. It's good to know that these organizations recognize that the mirroring of their client base is good for them and for business. So how does a certified business make its way into their supplier base?

We used to have a cartoon drawing on the company bulletin board. It was from a 1970s marketing book and featured an older, bald, grumpy-looking white man in a 1950s-style black suit and narrow tie. The caption was a bullet list:

- "I don't know who you are

- I don't know your company
- I don't know your products"

... and more, that concluded with "Now what did you want to sell me?" All business is about relationships, but how do we develop business relationships in the first place?

About a bazillion books, classes, and seminars are available on the topic, so this is not that, even though we do have something to say. Networking *is* working on your business, expanding its profile in specific communities, which is the fundamental criteria we use to determine whether to attend an event. We believe in taking the time to research the organizations who offer events. What is their charter and will it be mutually beneficial for our business to establish a relationship with this organization?

"Mutually beneficial?" you ask. Businesses have to be profitable, and many of these events are organized by nonprofits or government agencies, so fees are often associated with the event. Spend your money wisely with organizations you believe in so you'll both be viable for next year's big event. Attend events that allow you to make connections for future referrals. Seek or offer guidance on issues in your area of expertise. Learn how diverse procurements work with specific corporations or government agencies.

Showing up makes you and your company visible. Showing up often makes others more aware of your business. Contributing expertise or offering referrals makes you and your business memorable. Being memorable often leads to referrals and business for you. Schmooze, get to know people, especially purchasing and supplier diversity people who are likely to be your gateway into a potential business relationship with their organization. Get to know THEM, not just who they are and who they work for. Stay alert and observant, particularly if you are invited into someone's office. Noticing and asking about little details helps to connect as human beings, allowing you to build a relationship based on mutual respect and interest. Our best business relationships are with those people we have come to know on a personal, as well as business, level.

Don't, however, expect the world's Supplier Diversity Professionals (SDP) to applaud you for just showing up. Like us, they are imperfect humans doing the best they can at any given moment in time. And, the moment in time is important, particularly with regards to supplier diversity events. The smaller, local events draw hundreds of diverse business owners who are targeting a few dozen SDPs while national events draw thousands to meet with a few hundred. Even the best organized event is filled with distractions, bright lights, noises and people, *so many people*. Think about those SDPs and the formal match-making sessions:

- Will our fifteen-minute one-on-one meeting with an SDP be the first, fall in the middle, or be the last of the day?
- How many people want this person's attention today, right now?
- What kind of day are they having?
- Did they have any say in choosing who to meet with or was the match made by someone else?
- Is our commodity or service one their business has an interest in, ever? Are they familiar with how what we sell is purchased by their company?
- Do we all blur together in his or her mind at the end of the event, or did we do something memorable that made us stand out?

Many people like to complain and tell stories about outrageous SDP behavior, but that's not our point. If you're serious about growing your business you know that none of us should expect to close a sale with every contact we make. It seems unrealistic to expect SDPs to champion each of us. The matchmakers are akin to speed dating. You get an introduction, time for your best elevator pitch, a little Q&A, and a "thank you" on exit.

Sometimes, the follow up afterwards can be problematic. The SDP might not have buy-in from all sectors of the company, so even if they have need for your product or service, the buyer with authority might not care if it is procured from a diverse supplier. Other times, the need isn't current, and the SDP might suggest reaching out again months or even years (given the contract length) later. One SDP we know gets 75 to 100 blind approach emails a day (average 375 to 500) a week and over 22,750 per year), not to mention voice mail messages. So, even if they vividly remembers us, it could simply be that among all of the requests that they receive, ours gets lost in the shuffle—or accidentally filtered to a spam, junk or clutter folder. Lack of returned response is not necessarily a total lack of interest.

If an SDP tells you about a person to connect with in their organization, don't always expect them to make that introduction. Over and above all the diverse suppliers asking for a piece of the SDP's time, they are juggling their other job duties, supporting internal requests, attending meetings, traveling on business, filing reports or conducting research. Instead of waiting around for those introductions, take the initiative. Make note of the person mentioned and research him or her. When you reach out directly, copy the SDP and tell the contact that the SDP suggested there might be a synergy.

The one thing that we know works is personal persistence. Connecting with a supplier diversity professional on a personal level over a sustained period of time will get you noticed and remembered. If you are members of a third-party certifier, go to the events. These organizations are nonprofits and always in need of volunteers; giving a little of your time and expertise is a good way to be noticed in the community of partnering SDPs. Volunteering in general can facilitate relationships with target customers who have a culture of corporate responsibility. As Bob Burg, the author of a number of books on sales, marketing and influence, said, "Your true worth is determined by how much more you give in value than you take in payment." We need to make a difference in our communities, and who you serve/advocate/volunteer for may be as important as what you sell.

Beyond all that, remember that while SDPs want to facilitate the use of diverse suppliers, their priority is to do so in a manner that is in the best interest of their company. If the company is happy with their current provider and there is no inherent difference (innovation, quality or price) between it and the product or service we provide, it is unrealistic to expect a corporation to do business with us just because we're a diverse supplier. We have learned not to be afraid to recognize a real lack of opportunity; getting to a "no" faster frees up our time to seek a better "yes" elsewhere.

Certification & Government Contracting Relationships

On the other hand, certification and the lists of certified companies can be very important in government contracting. From municipalities to huge federal agencies, most contracts include diversity spend goals. The intent behind participation goals is to help diversely owned firms mature and grow our own capacity to directly support large companies and government agencies. A New York State comptroller's report says the programs are "intended to provide direct economic benefit to MWBE firms, as well as to increase the presence of these firms in the government contracting process, *thereby reversing the effects of direct or passive discriminatory practices present in many aspects of government procurement.*" This report goes on to declare, "Other analyses also indicate that minority- and women-owned businesses receive less than their fair share in the public contracting arena."

Certify and Sell

The power of government listings is arguably one of our most potent passive marketing tools. Each state has a search available to find their certified businesses. As more agencies and commercial enterprises commit to and actually track their diversity spending, these lists are invaluable to prime and sub-contractors. Our business has been certified by a number of states since the late 1980s, and we've noted a marked increase in the number of calls we receive from prime vendors who are bidding contracts in which we might not otherwise be able to participate.

That said, each contact represents its own unique challenges. Our first such experience happened back in 2001. A Virginia-based company was required to use a Missouri-certified WBE, and we had the appropriate skill-set to complete a discrete piece of the work. We entered into a contract, but as it continued, we were given very little work to do. At the end of the day, we were not compensated for the final portion of the project. This particular contract did not include much in the way of oversight with regard to compliance.

Having learned by doing in that instance, we've become more adept at reviewing potential bidding partnerships. Often, the conversations center on what goods and services we would provide. When it appears certain that we were contacted to perform as a pass-through so a prime could meet mandated diversity requirements, we find ourselves declining. If the intent is to help diverse companies grow, then simply providing a clerical service for invoicing and collecting funds doesn't strike us as meeting that intent. We want to actually perform a piece of the work. And, we have been successful in generating relationships with larger primes and other diverse companies in the commercial and government work we do.

We're on a second project with a major engineering firm that found us on the New York Empire State Development's WBE list. Participating in an Allegheny County, Pa., project as the mandated WBE led us to a direct, prime opportunity which we fulfilled in 2014. Recently, an Illinois procurement officer called to verify that our bid was, in fact, 75% WBE and 25% VBE ... we found the service-disabled veteran business on, that's right, the Illinois Business Enterprise Program's web published list.

When we began renovating a historic store front for our new office space, the very first thing we did was visit WBENC and our state disadvantaged business listings for prospective architects, general contractors, electricians, plumbers, elevator maintenance, and signage specialists because we believe we are stronger when we partner with other diverse certified businesses. If you are a certified diverse business, make sure your business's NAICS/UNSPC/SIC codes are correct and that you are listed on the certifier's website. Many companies will reach out to you to explore whether there are opportunities to partner.

It is practically free prospecting, so why not take full advantage?

But, beware the last-minute calls for diverse participation! There's barely a week the goes by that we don't get a participation inquiry. We're certified in many states, have a business name that appears near the top of the list and, though it pains us to say, many people are lazy when it comes to recruiting diverse partners. You know the ones where the proposal is due in three days and the vendor just realized diverse participation is mandatory, not just a goal. And, hey, they have to prove that no subcontractor, diverse or otherwise, can assist on the project.

One of the states that we support was acquiring new software, and only three major competitors were in this particular line of business. Because we read the RFP carefully, we knew who the agency was targeting— we targeted the vendor. Made an appointment, visited their offices, and came away shaking our heads. The vendor had never worked with subcontractors and wasn't about to start now. A few weeks before the proposal was due, they called. The state had convinced them they had to have MWBE participation or be disqualified. Our homework and past performance references with that state helped garner us a position on the contract, and the vendor has asked us to support them with another client.

Not all of these contacts have happy endings. Probably 20% come to fruition, but the longer the lead time, the more likely we are to develop a meaningful relationship with the prime vendor. We actually had a call from a vendor after a proposal was submitted. Nothing we said could convince this person that the state was serious about their mandatory participation, because he insisted they could not carve out work for a subcontractor. He called on a Thursday; the agency had given them until Monday to come up with an MWBE plan. Our guess, the agency ended up selecting another vendor.

Chapter 12: The Success of Others

The certification process began decades ago, established to verify that diverse businesses are legitimately diverse. Once simple, traveling the path to certification becomes more complex as time goes on. Many small or medium-sized businesses start but never complete their applications due to time constraints, missing materials, or feeling overwhelmed and losing interest because the value of certification can be unclear. To achieve a little clarity, we wanted to share the success of others so you can learn from what they have done.

Hannah Kain, President & CEO ALOM

(https://alom.com)

Hannah Kain knew at four that she wanted to run a company, an aspiration that came to fruition in 1997 when she founded ALOM. Kain's organization specializes in start-to-finish management and execution of global product supply chain management services, with sales and marketing operations. Kain wanted her company to be certified long before her 2002 WBENC certificate was awarded; however, the rules at the time required the business owner to be a U.S. citizen, and

118

having jumped the pond from Denmark, she only had a green card until 2001.

Like many people who get certified, she didn't have a particular return on her certification investment in mind and perhaps even thought that opportunities would fly in the window. In 2002, WBENC was still in its early days, and by getting involved from the beginning as an exhibitor and sponsor at events, Kain made many friends and established relationships with companies that were a good fit for her services. WBENC and its community, including WBEC Pacific and WBEC Great Lakes, have afforded her the opportunity to pay it forward with support, involvement, speaking, and mentorships. She also became aware of teaming opportunities with other diverse businesses, and ALOM is a founding member of Titanium Worldwide (www.titaniumww.com), which offers joint services to Fortune 100 companies, and continuously recruits certified minority, women, veteran, disabled, and LGBTQ companies to participate.

Kain says the hardest part of getting certified, beyond the huge number of copies that had to be made, was the convoluted process that was in place at the time. Her recommendation to business owners is to get certified early, always have your paperwork up-to-date and don't try any tricks. Like the stories of fraud earlier in this book, ALOM has discovered suppliers who are not quite who they say through its own supplier diversity program.

Because ALOM is supply chain management, her customers look to her for more than the widgets they deliver. Her supplier diversity program measures its spend and other metrics, not just on their own performance but performance by customers and sub-contractors to report to clients on tier levels 1, 2, and 3. Kain's program actually recruits as many qualified diverse businesses into its pipeline as it can, nurturing them and helping them grow and increase capacity for both ALOM and the diverse business.

Kain recommends that a diverse business should be selective about its approach. Find the companies that are a good fit for your goods and services where you can add value. In every case, you need to have a good value proposition to offer the potential customer, but one should be careful not to over-promise. Managing expectations and delivering your goods and services on time and on budget are important. (Kain, 2019)

Nora O'Hara, Manager EMR CPR LLC

(https://emrcpr.com/)

In 2016, Nora O'Hara was tasked with seeking certification for EMR CPR, then a three-year old IT solutions company owned by a pair of Hispanic American brothers. The NFL annually seeks local diverse suppliers for the Super Bowl; EMR CPR wanted to participate and needed to get certified quickly. O'Hara chose to apply for California's UCP. The Super Bowl vision remained a dream, but the DBE certification was awarded later that summer.

For O'Hara the most difficult aspect of certification was the site visit. As manager, she had to coordinate schedules with the two owners—each holds 50%, so both had to be present— and with the DOT's representative. At the time, EMR CPR ran a virtual office and leased storage facilities for its equipment, which led to an unusual request. The agency requested a second site visit at which time they shadowed EMR CPR at a client site to better understand how the company performed services for its clients. Subsequent to their California certification, EMR CPR decided to seek NMDC certification, which was awarded in 2019.

Certify and Sell

O'Hara suggests that companies serious about seeking certification work with an attorney or certification specialist. She believes spending the money for expert advice to make sure the application is completed correctly to be worthwhile. And, she stresses that if "you're a minority business, you should get certified." While O'Hara can't cite specific certification-related contracts, she finds the networking opportunities to be valuable for EMR CPR and notes that they are reaping indirect benefits. Team members have attended local supplier diversity events and went to 2019's national NMSDC conference in Atlanta. The company is now able to participate in bidding MWBE opportunities that were previously unavailable to them, and ultimately, it is just a matter of time until EMR CPR wins some MWBE contracts. (O'Hara, 2020)

Richard W. Taylor, CEO IMBUTEC

(http://www.imbutec.com)

Currently in their sixth year as an 8(a) firm, Richard Taylor's IMBUTEC is certified by NMSDC, Pennsylvania's Unified Certification Program (with reciprocal certificates in Ohio and Maryland) and verified as a Minority Business Enterprise by the Pennsylvania Department of General Services. IMBUTEC performs a variety of general and electrical construction services, leading Taylor to seek certification because he recognized it as a necessity for certain opportunities. Taylor thought that certification would put IMBUTEC on the road to success and contracts would rain down on them, but the reality was different.

While third-party certification, like NMSDC, might more quickly ready you for action with supplier diversity corporates, and while government certificates get you on lists, you still have to cultivate and build meaningful relationships with your targeted customers. Taylor says business owners need to understand that certification is a tool that complements what you offer. He spoke about the mistake most certified businesses make when we misread the landscape expecting that supplier diversity representatives make the purchases. They don't. They are the internal advocates who will tell you the truth about what's going on in that corporation.

For example, NMSDC facilitates the networking with supplier diversity and supplier diversity can help you decode the matrix of that corporation's business. Some supplier diversity people are extremely helpful, and building the right relationship can help you figure out who to talk to so you can talk about your capabilities to the right end client. The business owner needs to instill confidence in his or her supplier diversity representative so they will want to take you to the buyers. The Office of Small and Disadvantaged Business Utilization (OSDBU) is similar to supplier diversity, and following the pattern of relationship development with OSDBU staff is critical to learning how to make that sale.

Even in today's more diverse and inclusive world, Taylor reminds us that we must overcome all kinds of ghosts. The "old boys" network that doesn't expect to see people of color or women in charge. The pass-through fraud companies that did not deliver. The institutional barriers that expect you to fail because they think "small, certified" is code for unable to compete or perform. Taylor quoted his father, "You can't come back from where you've never gone," so go forward, eyes wide open, to make certification work for your business. (Taylor, 2019)

Gabrielle Christman, Hunter International Recruiting

(https://hirecruiting.com/)

It is no surprise that Gabrielle Christman is an entrepreneur, growing up with grandparents and parents who trod the entrepreneurial trail. Christman started Hunter International Recruiting in 2006. Hunter International focuses on STEM (science, technology, engineering, and math) recruiting for some of the world's largest companies. She has "a passion for connecting clients with the best and brightest STEM talent in their industry."

As a fierce advocate for women in business, Christman planned to get certified from the very beginning. It took a year before she could apply to WBENC, the largest third-party certifier of WBEs, because the rules at the time required at least one year of a business's financial reports. In 2007, Christman was on the phone with a huge client she'd been courting who wanted to know if she and her business were certified. She had to report that they were in the process, but when she hung up the phone, she found her certificate waiting in her email. That client received immediate notice, and the die was cast. Christman's return on investment happened even faster than she expected. And, today, about 85% of her clients would be upset if she let her certificate expire.

Christman's strategy is to begin most conversations about Hunter International by letting people know it is 100% women-owned and operated and in STEM. In an era where the news is filled with articles about how few women enter and stay in STEM, it is a big differentiator for her company. Certification is embedded in Hunter's corporate identity, values, and branding. She grows that recognition by working with other WBEs and actively participating in the Ohio River Valley council's events and WBENC's national events.

For Christman, finding the time to apply for certification was an issue. In the beginning, she was the only employee. Gathering the documents and understanding and completing the forms in an era with little online support required a commitment. This commitment had a direct impact on the business because that meant it was time away from sales and recruiting, the way she made her living. For new businesses considering certification, Christman says "take the time to figure out your priorities before you start the application" because if you want it to be successful for your business "what you put in is what you get out." So, she coaches other women who want to own businesses to help impact the next generation of strong WBEs. (Christman, 2020)

Tracy Paonessa, Owner J.P. Investigative Group, Inc.

(www.jpinvestigations.com)

Tracy Paonessa, like many business owners, was set on the path to certification by a customer at the end of 2018. The customer was aware that excellent services were being delivered by a WBE, but they couldn't recognize their expenditures in meeting their diversity goals because her company wasn't certified. Paonessa ended up with five certifications: WBENC, the SBA's WOSB, North Carolina UCP and HUB, along with Pennsylvania's UCP certificates.

She initially expected a better return on investment, because state-funded RFPs are highly interested in Paonessa's offerings in surveillance and special investigations around potential fraud in worker's comp, disability, and procurement, as well as pre-employment services. However, she found that many of these requests ended up awarding contracts to multiple companies, producing a "round robin" methodology of actual assignments, which while helping to grow the business, is not as profitable as initially expected.

Paonessa's strategy is to look for the requests that put an emphasis on minority and disadvantaged business enterprise participation; and, she has seen a growth in the number of contracts awarded. How this will ultimately impact her overall revenue stream is yet to be determined.

Paonessa says the process and paperwork was the most difficult part of her certification journey. The company was founded in 2000, so some missing, old, paperwork had to be accounted for. And who keeps cancelled checks or receipts for longer than the seven-year tax requirements anyway? But those hurdles were overcome.

If you are beginning the certification process, Paonessa says, "Be aware that just because you receive the certifications, the business will not come to you. You will still have to market your business and research opportunities." And she recommends that, once awarded, you let your existing customers know when you get certified because that may open more doors where you already do business.

Joining webinars for events that are relevant to her business with the certifiers is one way Paoenssa gets to know supplier diversity representatives and other diverse business owners. She also attends industry-related conferences, four to six annually, at least once per quarter. (Paonessa, 2020)

Earl Mann; President OQ Point, LLC

(www.oqpoint.com)

Earl Mann's story is different, because his approach to certification was vastly divergent from the other stories we collected. Previously involved with other business entities,

Mann actually acquired a business with an infrastructure and past performance that he could get certified. It was clear to him that certification would help him focus on a specific market, help him establish credibility and, ultimately, help him work with companies that have already invested in the diverse community. Mann chose to work with a professional certification consultant, and his company is certified by NMSDC, the Department of Veteran's Affairs (VA), his home state's UCP program (with seven reciprocal state certificates) and NVBDC.

His expected return on this investment was "a license to hunt," which he has used to register in supplier diversity portals before beginning his networking efforts. Mann's philosophy and approach have yielded rewards: in three years, he has managed to secure 50 master service agreements, and 100% of his company's revenues are attributable to one or more of his certifications.

The hardest part of getting certified for Mann was gathering the information to get started. He discovered that outside counsel was critical because he didn't want to spend the time learning how to get certified. He recommends that business owners "be in business before certifying ... don't certify as, say a veteran, certify as an XYZ business that happens to be veteran-owned." Working out the kinks of delivering your business's goods or services before getting certified will give you what you need—"an accelerant to marketing or more chances to do what you do." Especially, as Mann does, through networking at local, regional and national diversity events. (Mann, 2020)

John Scifers; President SCIGON

(https://www.scigon.com)

Back in 2000, John Scifers was job hunting when the veteran's representative at his UC office introduced him to Donald C. Richards who was a Senior Vice President of Leo Burnett Worldwide. Leo Burnett was pursuing a $300 million advertising contract with the DOD that included a service-disabled veteran-owned small business (SDVOSB) goal. Unable to find an existing company with Scifers' skillset, Richards "took me by the hand and walked me through forming a business, certification, and the basics of federal contracting." Scifers could not have had a better introduction! Richards, himself, was the first African American vice president managing Leo Burnett's global diversity program before becoming the associate national director of affirmative action and diversity for the New York-based Screen Actors Guild.

They didn't win the contract, but Richards and Leo Burnett Worldwide gave Scifers the tools to start his first business. His initial VA certification was, he says, "incredibly easy." Unfortunately, it was so easy at the time that many companies fraudulently applied for and received certification. By his next time around, the VA had done a 180 and turned it into an incredibly difficult process, so much so that SCIGON was initially rejected. Several thousands of dollars in legal fees and a great deal of time was expended before SCIGON earned its rightful certification.

The VA, at that time, had implemented a strident process that overwhelmed its own analysts and adjudicators, so much so that they confused Scifers' IT background with a demolition company and cited a lack of his demolition experience as a reason for denial. Scifers has a strong sense of humor when he says, "While blowing stuff up sounds like fun, I never had that experience, let alone putting it on my resume … and this was just one of several errors in that rejection letter." *Note*: the VA process changed again in 2019 and has become more consistent with other federal programs.

The experience of working with Leo Burnett Worldwide on starting his business and seeking that contract taught Scifers his biggest lesson—to aim high. SCIGON is certified in multiple states (Illinois, Missouri, New York, Ohio, Pennsylvania, and Virginia) and the City of Chicago. He uses these certificates to market his business. He finds that it is "a way in, an introduction that allows them to grow within the Fortune 100 network." About 20% of SCIGON's volume can be directly related to SDVOSB certification.

Scifers' advice to other vets about certification is about leverage. Make sure you have educated yourself on using that certification in the public sector, building a business and marketing plan to identify your best opportunities. "Make sure to align with other organizations in your socio-equity category" because many public offerings seek a coalition of diverse talent to deliver. And, as much as we all complain, "Supplier Diversity Portals can be our friends!" (Scifers, 2020)

Janeen Zook; CEO Trattativa Meetings and Event Management

(https://www.trattativameetings.com/)

When Janeen Zook started her event planning business in 2007, supplier diversity wasn't even on her radar. She'd come out of corporate America with expertise in media and event planning and an entrepreneurial spirit. Three-and-a-half years later, Zook met a fellow businesswoman whose company she engaged in support of a client. The next day, Zook found herself invited to a WBEC West (WBENC's regional partner on the West Coast) networking event. It was a revelatory experience, to meet other women business owners with whom she could build relationships. Initially, the hardest part was showing up not knowing anyone. For the next year-and-a-half, Zook went to every WBEC West/WBENC event she could before tackling the somewhat intimating certification process.

She says the paperwork really isn't as intimidating as it looks. Zook suggests that tackling it, organizing your supporting materials, and knowing your books are in order will help you have good habits. It helped her grow from a single person firm into a large business supporting major national clients.

Once certified, Zook got involved because "nothing is free. If you want something, you have to work for it." She grew both personally and professionally, building confidence and doing business with other women-owned companies—98% of Trattativa buys come from other diverse businesses. Zook volunteers at many WBEC West and WBENC events, speaks on panels and has served on the WBENC Forum. She has taken advantage of the education available through WBENC's IBM Tuck Executive program and one offered through Wells Fargo. Zook has assisted the WBEC West Council with its regional events since 2012 and recently won the contract for WBENC's Summit & Salute and national conference events through 2022. (Zook, 2019)

Blanca Robinson; Viva Consulting Group

(http://www.vivaconsultinggroup.net/)

Blanca Robinson has seen both sides of certification, spending 17 years with the Women's Business Enterprise Council—South, which is a WBENC regional partner organization based in Metairie, La. Robinson came from the oil and gas industry into a fledgling nonprofit. She was their first employee working out of donated space—an empty room with tables, chairs, book cases, and four or five banker boxes of file folders. With a small, but supportive board, the council boasted seventy-five WBEs four years later.

Having laid out yet another growth plan for a WBE, Robinson had her own "aha moment' and started Viva Consulting Group upon her retirement in 2016, becoming WBENC-certified immediately. To those seeking certification, Robinson says the certificate is a marketing tool, but it also connects WBEs to other like-minded women and gives validity that the organization has passed muster and is legitimately women-owned and operated. She encourages all WBEs to certify and join the shared experience. Witnessing the comingling of third-party certifiers at the 2019 WBENC National Conference, Robinson says she would love to see more reciprocity amongst the organizations (WBENC, NMSDC, NVBDC, NGLCC, DisabilityIN, and NaVOBA). (Robinson, 2019)

Chapter 13: Sharing and Connecting

Have you ever played "Six Degrees of Kevin Bacon"? It's a game based on the "six degrees of separation" concept that says any two people on Earth can be connected through six or fewer acquaintances. In the Kevin Bacon game, you try to link other actors to the prolific Bacon. In 2007, Bacon turned the game into a nonprofit that uses everyday activities to connect people and causes (check it out at www.sixdegrees.org). We digress because we believe that six degrees can, and should, apply in our own diverse relationships. And, we've seen it work in several ways.

Marian recently graduated from the Small Business Administration's Emerging Leaders program, and whenever something comes across her desk, whether it's a networking or educational event for her cohort to attend or request for proposal that is specific to one of her classmates, she shares it. In 2018, the Emerging Leaders program piloted an alumni program, which rolled out nationwide in 2019. This initiative allows for all the local alums to connect with each other, widening their pool of resources to tap into. As Marian likes to say, "You never know where your next lead will come from."

We helped a company in New York with pre-certification advice on their organizing documents and consequently learned a little about their business. It was just enough that when we saw an RFP posted for retirement fund management, we thought of them and forwarded the announcement. A few months later, we got a thank you email because they had won the contract.

A company referred to us by the local SBA Women's Business Center became a certification client that we helped get third-party and state certified. They do title searches and other property sales related services, but they are known for hiring and training veterans. Because we get all the notices from Virginia, we shared a request about title searches with them and, that's right, they too won a contract.

For years Pittsburgh didn't have much activity when it came to women in business, so we put together an informal group of ladies who brunch (or breakfast, have cocktails, whatever). It started with six or seven business owners and has grown to over 100 of us who get together monthly. It grew because we're relaxed, and we talk about our business issues in meaningful ways. But most importantly, at every meeting, we each get one "ask." Yes, it is often a request for leads, but there is a tendency to ask for other types of assistance.

Certify and Sell

A lawyer once asked whether a small monthly retainer would be attractive so we'd always have someone to ask legal advice of—a resounding "yes" from the group. A CPA owner was struggling with an employee who always left at 5 p.m. during tax season—the group advised that they find out if this person wanted a job or career because they were letting the whole group down during peak season. We requested an introduction to a member of the Mayor of Pittsburgh's staff so we could court him to compete with the Mayor of Reno in a new socially responsible venture with us. Our group is committed to helping each other succeed. And many of these relationships go beyond the monthly meeting. One attendee is our attorney, another the graphic design and marketing team we use, and a third is our printer.

The point is, as a member of the diverse business community, you'll come across opportunities that aren't right for you. But if you take a moment or two, you likely know someone who might be thrilled to know about it. We often just forward the email or link with the comment "not sure if this is of interest, but thought of you" and push it along. If we do this often enough, it will come back.

For us it has. One of our favorite people, who never bought what we sell, used to represent another large WBE firm. She is always referring people to our certification practice (for which we are deeply grateful!). In one case, there was an investigative firm they wanted to use, women-owned but not certified. We helped the company get certified by WBENC, the state of North Carolina, and the Commonwealth of Pennsylvania. The relationship didn't end there. We were asked to be the WBE supplier on an Illinois project that required us to have background checks conducted on the people we assigned. And, we just happened to know a recently certified investigator. We think this might have been three degrees of separation, but who's actually counting?

Chapter 14: Third-Party Certifiers

The MBDA (Minority Business Development Agency) was established as part of the U.S. Department of Commerce by Nixon's 1969 Executive Order 11625 (Nixon R. M., 1969). It was created "to assist minority businesses in achieving effective and equitable participation in the American free enterprise system and in overcoming social and economic disadvantages that have limited their participation in the past." (Minority Business Development Agency, 2019)· In 1972, National Minority Supplier Development Council (NMSDC) was founded as the National Minority Purchasing Council (NMPC). With federal funding, its mission was "to pursue the single objective of encouraging major corporations to adopt and implement programs to increase their purchases of goods and services from minority businesses." It eventually became a self-supporting organization, dropping its federal funding. (National Minority Supplier Development Council, 2018)

Although NMSDC was established to assist minority-owned firms, it certified and represented women-owned companies (WBEs) as members until 1992 when non-minority women-owned companies were given notice that they would be disaffiliated. The WBEs were stunned by their expulsion, potential loss of certification and the severing of relationships with corporate supplier diversity programs.

A handful of Dallas-based women used government statistics and reports to illustrate how the disaffiliation excluded WBEs and made the heartfelt case for WBE inclusion in procurement and employment opportunities. Well organized, in 1994 they succeeded in getting 18 corporations to sign a women's covenant that set goals to "result in the expansion of economic opportunities for all women, regardless of ethnic background," with requirements for annual reporting.

In February 1995, NMSDC declared that there should be two distinct, separate organizations. The women were concerned, but in March, funding had been pledged and the fledgling Texas Women's Business Council opened in summer 1995. By 1997, they negotiated a national structure providing reciprocal certification, education, and networking with 12 women's councils as the Women's Business Enterprise National Council (WBENC). (WBENC, 1992)

All of the third-party certifiers share similar definitions when it comes to the owners and businesses each certifies. Just like government certification requirements, the business must be

51% owned, governed, and controlled by members of the community that the certifier serves—one may certify and serve minorities, another women, etc. They, too, have rules about independence, citizenship, and being organized for profit. The biggest difference is size-related. A third-party certified business doesn't age out or become too large to participate.

So how do these groups operate, and what do they do on behalf of their certified members?

NMSDC

NMSDC was the first U.S. third-party certifier, originally known as National Minority Purchasing Council, established in 1972. Headquartered in New York City, it has 23 affiliate councils in this country and is associated with the Global Supplier Diversity Alliance, which has a presence in Australia, Canada, China, South Africa, and the United Kingdom.

To be certified by NMSDC, the business must be at least 51% owned by ethnic minorities who are U.S. citizens. With the exception of veteran-based certifications, NMSDC is the only certifier that requires U.S. citizenship. Most government and other certifiers accept applications from companies owned by U.S. permanent residents, people who have been granted the right to live in the United States indefinitely. NMSDC recognizes ethnic minorities: African American, Asian American, Hispanic American, Native American including Pacific Islanders, and Subcontinent Asian American. In 2017, the organization had about 12,000 certified firms with 72% male and 28% female ownership. At that time, it had 1,595 participating corporations, 430 of whom are national NMSDC partners with 1,165 others at the regional or local level.

Despite multiple attempts, we were unable to connect with NMSDC officials. We would have liked to ask them about its future plans regarding proof of ethnicity. Its website indicates that "There is a stark difference between *knowing* that you are an ethnic or racial minority" and "*demonstrating through documentation* that you are one. The most common way for applicants to demonstrate their ethnic or racial background is by producing the birth certificate or death certificate of a parent or grandparent during the certification process." As the pool of business owners seeking certification gains more generations between themselves and those born before the Civil War, we're curious what NMSDC will do when the minimum 25% ethnicity can't be proven with a birth certificate. Visit NMSDC.org to learn more.

Certify and Sell

WBENC

WBENC was born in 1997, when fourteen national corporate founding partners came together with twelve regional partner organizations (RPOs). As of 2020, there were 15,768 WBENC certified women-owned businesses with 318 corporate and government partners. Of the certified businesses, 6,314 achieved women-owned small business (WOSB) certification, according to U.S. federal standards.

While vice president of Pfizer's Worldwide Procurement, Pamela Prince-Eason, Pfizer appointed her to serve on WBENC's Board, where she developed a full understanding of diversity and inclusion. At the time, Prince-Eason had responsibility for procurement outside the U.S. Pfizer's diversity was literally everything, and its inclusion practices were different in every country. The insights she gained helped "develop my passion for being part of opening up large business supply chains to smaller business." Prince-Eason became WBENC's third president in March 2011.

WBENC's national review committee manages, reviews, and updates certification standards. It has a subcommittee to evaluate the applications of exceptional WBEs, over $500 million for very complex organizations. The appeals committee is responsible for reviews when a denial is challenged. In 2006, WBENC conducted internal reviews to verify that all updates and new DOT rules were incorporated into WBENC's 2.0 rules. The alignment with DOT standards made it possible to negotiate with states to accept the WBENC certificate. With an established International Organization of Standards-type of process, WBENC standards are consistently applied across all the RPOs. Once an application is received, it is reviewed by the RPO's staff members for completeness. Missing documents or information is requested, and once complete, the RPO's Certification Committee reviews the full application package and schedules an onsite visit. The committee, and its site visitors, is made up of corporate member-certified WBE, government agency, and/or community advocate representatives.

Under Prince-Eason's tenure, WBENC has experienced three recent rule changes. Two happened in 2011. The first reduced the time for denied applicants to reapply from 1 year to 6 months. The second was to become a third-party certifier for the SBA's WOSB certification, which increases opportunities for WBEs navigating the private and public sector for contracts. In 2015, WBENC changed its trust criteria which were more lenient to female business owners who have used estate planning and incorporated it into their business.

Certify and Sell

Opportunities come in many forms, and WBENC's CORE (certification, opportunities, resources, engagement) mission facilitates multiple approaches. Engagement involves 650 to 750 events annually—local, regional and national—bringing together corporate and WBE members for networking and educational opportunities. The two national events, Summit and Salute and its National Conference and Business Fair (NCBF), rotate around the United States with different themes each year to assist members in their success.

Engagement as a participant or volunteer is a critical component of opportunity. One message Prince-Eason wants to convey to WBEs is "being granted certification does not constitute a guarantee of business. Business owners must become involved in the WBENC network to maximize their opportunities. People do business with people they *know*." (Prince-Eason, 2020)

NGLCC

Justin Nelson cofounded the National LGBT Chamber of Commerce (NGLCC) with Chance Mitchell in 2002 to advocate on behalf of LGBTQ business owners. The chamber serves as a voice promoting the interests of its members and celebrating their impact on the U.S. economy. The chamber began its journey in the shadow of 9/11, during the "don't ask don't tell" years, in advance of great political change.

By 2007, the chamber had established necessary partnerships to begin its program, which now represents over 250 corporate partners and over 1200 certified businesses. Continuously engaging with partners and members by conducting supplier boot camps, coaching for matchmakers, providing materials for employee or business resource groups (ERG/BRGs) and an annual conference is how the NGLCC delivers value.

The NGLCC procurement committee is responsible for certification rules and has approved a few rule changes, particularly around status qualifiers, and accepted supporting documents such as marriage and divorce decrees. The process itself lies with a centralized certification committee with a team of analysts reviewing applications and regional assets conducting site visits. The chamber introduced the two-year certificate while continuing to require an annual affidavit.

When asked about deciding to pursue certification, Nelson suggests that business owners define ideal clients and then look at the affiliated partners list as potential doors the chamber can help you open. "Don't expect a contract," he says. "Certification is an entry into the marathon. And, don't overlook the other members. It is a whole network of potential clients." (Nelson, 2020)

Disability:IN

Disability:IN's roots were planted by a President George H. W. Bush-era President's Committee on Employment of People with Disabilities. Tasked with expanding employment opportunities for people with disabilities (PWDs), Chair Tony Coelho allocated funds and staff for the Business Leadership Network (BLN), which joined the private sector in 2002 as a 501 (C) (3) nonprofit: the U.S. Business Leadership Network (USBLN).

The USBLN's Disability Supplier Diversity Program was launched in 2010, just a few years before the renaming/rebranding to Disability:IN which "empowers business to achieve disability inclusion and equality." Working with champions at Ernst Young, Freddie Mac, IBM, Marriott, Microsoft, Southwest Airlines, and Sun Trust, board members determined a DOBE certification would help further its goals for expanding disability inclusion.

Following best practices, Disability:IN developed a program similar to other third-party certifiers. It involves an application process to demonstrate that the company is owned, operated, and controlled by a person(s) with a disability. The supporting documents are different in that the applicant must submit a doctor's form that confirms the owner(s) is a member of the disability community. An analyst reviews the application to make sure it is complete with all supporting materials and brings it to the committee for review. Once reviewed, a site visit is scheduled, and its results are returned to the committee for final determination.

Today, Disability:IN has a huge list of corporate members and over 200 certified businesses. (Turcotte, 2019)

NaVOBA

National Veteran-Owned Business Association (NaVOBA) began as a publishing company with a mission to serve U.S. veteran entrepreneurs in 2007. With corporate spokesperson Rocky Bleier—himself an iconic Pittsburgh story of persistence fighting through a service-acquired disability to play with the Steelers again—its mission was to promote the employment of veterans, publishing informational articles supported by job advertising. Corporate allies began asking NaVOBA to consider offering a certification program so allies would be able to count and track NaVOBA certified members against their diversity spend. Modeled on the successful programs at

Certify and Sell

WBENC and NMSDC, NaVOBA began certifying Veteran and Service-Disabled Veteran Owned Businesses in 2017.

Before you can begin the certification process, NaVOBA asks you to create a TroopID/ID.me login specifically tied to NaVOBA. When you complete this step, the interface between NaVOBA and the VA actually verifies the veteran status of the owner creating an account. While you're asked to provide an official discharge document, you've already been appropriately vetted.

Mimi Lohm, Vice President of Corporate Relations and Chief Development Officer, recommends that veterans considering certification take the time to read about NaVOBA on their website so they understand the tools and processes before starting the journey. Gathering the documentation and submitting an application is just the beginning. Achieving certification, Lohm says, "doesn't mean you're more qualified. It's just a marketing tool." The VBE owner should know his or her value proposition, what they can do for their customers, and be prepared to discuss that rather than announcing they are certified. (Lohm, 2019)

NVBDC

Keith King's motivation in founding the National Veteran Business Development Center (NVBDC) is a series of stories about fraud and lack of corporate due diligence, particularly centered on VBEs. First, we need to understand the definition of a veteran: one who is a former member of the Armed Forces of the United States (Army, Navy, Air Force, Marine Corps, and Coast Guard) who served on active duty and was discharged under conditions that were other than dishonorable. (Reservists called to active duty by executive order qualify as veterans.) This definition is the founding principle of NVBDC.

It seems pretty simple, but the VA does not certify VBE companies, it merely verifies that the company is owned and operated by a veteran. And, the VA is the only federal agency that requires a VA verification. *"The Vets First Verification Program affords verified firms owned and controlled by Veterans and Service-disabled Veterans the opportunity to compete for VA set asides."*

Even more interesting is that the original 1999 law told the secretary to verify the information in the VA's database, not the veteran's status. So, technically, a record of service with no active service or a dishonorable discharge could absolutely be correct but would not establish the veteran's bona fides. The process for the CVE (Center for Verification and Evaluation) mandated in 2006 was not created until 2008.

King's experience in procurement got him invited to look at how the CVE was rolled out and exposed him to some interesting challenges. For example, a large company was awarded a huge contract that entailed 30% diverse spend. Less than 6 years ago, this federal prime went back to the end client saying they couldn't find any diverse businesses to perform the work. As a test for himself, King found verifiably competent MBE partners in three weeks, WBE partners in six, and VBE partners in about eight. But the powers that be waived about $240 million in diversity spend that could not be protested because, to protest an award, you must have standing—in this case, be one of the bidders. This became the impetus for NVBDC.

Establishing NVBDC in 2014, King went to certification school, learning from his counterparts at WBENC and NMSDC. At a very fortunate time, King had the opportunity to create a different version of a similar story as it applied to veteran-owned businesses. In this organization, the certification process may involve a legal review of bylaws and operating agreements, and the organization's treasurer is a forensic accountant. All veterans, by the way.

As a third-party certifier of veteran and service-disabled veteran owned businesses, NVBDC has a unique twist. It requires that the DD214, the official documentation used by the U.S. military organizations, be submitted to them by the U.S. military organization(s) itself. Initially, we questioned this extra burden of proof requirement levied against veterans, until King suggested that we Google "blank DD214 forms." Over 34,000 hits and a little further reading taught us how easily someone could fake a DD214 form and lots of ways to tell how a person might be faking his or her service.

The NVBDC team works with its certified Veteran Businesses to create strong, well-written capability statements, which have proven to be one of the steps needed for success. Many of its corporate members believe that the best way to build capacity is to get into their supplier program and, when awarded an opportunity, that our veterans "under promise and over deliver." NVBDC recommends doing the job on time, on budget and exceeding all quality standards. "If they do that, the repeat orders will come, and they will be on the right path to capacity building and sustainability," King says.

Certify and Sell

In December 2018, NVBDC had 500 certified SD/VOBs and over 70 corporate members. (King, 2019)

Chapter 15: Intersectionality

Intersectionality is a big word we're hearing around the diverse community these days. Kimberlé Crenshaw coined the word to demonstrate that "[b]ecause the intersectional experience is greater than the sum of racism and sexism, any analysis that does not take intersectionality into account cannot sufficiently address the particular manner in which Black women are subordinated." (Crenshaw, 2019) In our supplier diversity and certification world, the term is often used to describe diverse suppliers who hold multiple certifications.

Our company holds four major certifications, being certified by our state's UCP as a DBE, the SBA as an SBE and a WOSB, WBENC as a WBE, and Disability:IN as a DOBE. One of our clients is a minority veteran-owned company holding VA, NVBDC, NMSDC, and several state DBE certifications. Another is a service-disabled veteran certified by the VA and NaVOBA and registered as an SBA Small Business Enterprise. Our customers—corporations or government agencies—can choose how to count the dollars they spend with us based on the rule of their organization. If they're short in disability spending, our DOBE certificate makes us eligible. Maybe they really need WBEs. We've got that, too. The point is that having multiple ways to add value for our clients through a variety of certificates affords us the opportunity to open more doors through our marketing. If you and your business legitimately qualify for multiple types of certification, both you and your customers may find that to be mutually beneficial.

Intersectionality and NBIC

Spearheaded by the NGLCC, the US-based National Business Inclusion Consortium (NBIC) unites leading business diversity organizations. "The NBIC encourages parity in cross-segment diversity and inclusion initiatives in corporate America, works to identify areas of collaboration among diverse businesses, and advocates for the advancement of policies that support the growth of diverse-owned companies in both the public and private sectors." (Corporate Relations, 2019) And, its Best-of-the-Best event recognizes outstanding achievement in promoting cross-segment diversity and inclusion. Members include National LGBT Chamber of Commerce (NGLCC); Disability:IN; National Minority Supplier Development Council (NMSDC); National Veteran-Owned Business Association (NaVOBA); U.S. Black Chambers, Inc. (USBC); United States Hispanic Chamber of Commerce (USHCC); United States Pan Asian American Chamber of Commerce

(USPAAC); WEConnect International; Women Impacting Public Policy (WIPP); and WBENC.

Chapter 16: Disparity Studies

Diverse spend goals differ from state to state and regionally. For example, Illinois has a 19% MWBE spend goal, Missouri 15% and Texas 13%. (Insight Center for Community Economic Development, 2017) Have you ever wondered how these diverse spend goals are set? Lots of government studies and interviews called Disparity Studies are conducted to determine what the utilization of DMWBE should be by various states, counties, and cities.

Any study generally examines the process for attaining products and services, the subcontracting practices of prime contractors/service providers who do business with the government, and the evidence collected from a broad cross-section of DMWBE and non-DMWBE firms. The studies usually evaluate goals established by federal, state, and local governments and help these agencies develop effective and lawful affirmative action programs for procuring goods and services from businesses owned by minorities and women.

A number of states wrapped up their disparity studies in 2019. They wanted to learn how their MWBEs (Minority and Women Business Enterprises) have fared under their programs — to see if there has been a net positive impact of

MWBE business contracting. As a certified DWBE in 26 states, we participated in several over the last couple of years. The great majority were simple online surveys about our experiences in contracting with their particular state government and soliciting comments about how the program could be improved. In Maryland, however, we participated in one of several actual interview processes held around the state. It was eye-opening in many ways.

Maryland's interviews were segmented by business type. We fell into the category of "Other Professional & General Services" and spent two hours in a room of 50 or so service providers for the interview. What we learned was that construction-related business and commodities providers are doing quite well, and their success is often the reason many constituents think Disadvantaged and MWBE programs have fulfilled their mission and that the state should consider retiring the program. On the other hand, professional services have had almost polar opposite experiences, and their lack of representation in diversity dollar spend is cited as a primary reason for keeping the program. One thing everyone in the room agreed upon: a disconnect lies between contract goals/awards and the actual work done/paid for, or compliance. And, primes seem to suffer no consequences if they fail to comply with the terms and conditions of diverse business enterprise use.

Our favorite moment, however, came from the devil's advocate sitting next to us. She asked whether the MWBE companies in the room had a diverse staff. She wanted to know if their diversity and inclusion practices had resulted in an employee population that mirrored the state's population statistics. We came away with that comment resonating deeply. In fact, our own organization doesn't reflect the Pennsylvania population. Though our MBE and VBE employees outnumber the two Caucasian males and two Caucasian females, we are under-represented in the Hispanic and Native American categories. Now we're thinking about how to address that issue internally.

Our takeaway from disparity studies? Yes, we still need programs that encourage the use of small diverse suppliers in state and federal contracting opportunities. But, a bigger issue is that we diverse business owners should give more thought to how our own human resource recruitment procedures might be changed to diversify our own workforce.

Disparity and the Future

The millennial generation, considered to be those born between 1981 and 1996, now 44% minority, is the most diverse adult generation in American history. Raised in the multicultural world connected by social media, the 75 million millennials may not realize that systemic discriminatory gaps exist in contracting, which can prevent diverse companies from pursuing potential opportunities. Millennials don't consider diversity as only demographics. They tend to have a broader definition that includes:

- Tolerance, inclusiveness, and openness (18%)
- Respect and acknowledgment of the individual (17%)
- Different ideas or ways of thinking (14%)

The Deloitte study states that "diversity/inclusion and flexibility are important keys to keeping [millennials] happy." (Cotteleer, 2017) So how will that fit into a supplier diversity model? Ultimately, as the data gets better, it will become possible to look at disparity and availability when setting contracting goals.

Chapter 17: Marketing with Your Certification

The main thing about marketing with your certification is to not lead with it. While that sounds counter-intuitive, every single certifier and supplier diversity person we speak with reminds us that the certificate is a value add. That means you must have a product or service that stands on its own. It is your ability to deliver solutions with excellent customer service/support that potential clients care about. *Certification is icing on the cake.*

For example, we recently conducted a presentation to a state agency. We spoke for about 45 minutes about the service and how it was offered, and the agency was interested because it would save them money. In discussing the next steps, we mentioned that we were certified as a DBE by their state DOT program. The conversation got even more intense as we were asked to send out our overall capability statement and a copy of the certificate ASAP. The client contact said, "There may be other projects we want to discuss with you." In this case, the certification may open additional doors for us.

That said, you can use your certification as a marketing tool. Particularly in taking advantage of networking or meet-and-greet events sponsored by certifiers, prime contractors, nonprofits, and government agencies. Participation and volunteerism will help you develop the personal relationships that may eventually turn into opportunities. Companies are comprised of people. People have a tendency to do business with those they know and trust. Use your certification to become known and trusted.

Just being on the various state lists has been a great passive marketing tool for Abator. We began marketing to state government agencies in the early 1990s and discovered that they had goals for MWBE participation. We also learned that they could only count what they spent with companies who were certified in their state. This is how our initial certification strategy came to be, identifying the states where we wanted to do business. What we didn't realize until recently was how many large primes don't have relationships with certified subcontractors. Those calls we talked about getting in chapter eleven are a direct result of this strategy. We're on the list when primes are looking, and you will be too, if you get state certified. It's a good idea to be prepared for those calls and emails; maybe even have a routine you follow to explores working with the caller's company.

Preparing for Primes

Ask about the RFP and when it's due. If it is less than a week, this prime isn't likely to be looking to develop a relationship with you and your business, they need to check off a box and get it checked off quickly.

Ask what work you and your company would be expected to perform. Legitimately, your contact might not know. They have probably been handed a list and told to find a vendor. This is where knowing something about the RFP comes in handy. But, even if you are both a little clueless at this point, you can figure it out by asking what the prime is doing on the project. If they are building bridges and you supply concrete or rebar, this could be a match made in heaven. On the other hand, if your product is office supplies you would have to come up with a creative way to be included. It is best to be less creative when trying to be an MWBE subcontractor.

If it is a good match, you'll likely need to get a mutual teaming or non-disclosure agreement together pretty quickly. As the subcontractor, there are immediate things to look for, even before you ask your attorney to review the paperwork. You want to make sure that the agreement doesn't prevent you from marketing your goods and services. We always make sure that any language on this topic is limited to the specific client and project named in the RFP, and/or the institutions and people the prime introduces us to during the lifetime of the agreement. It doesn't make sense for a company to give up trying to sell in the state Michigan if the prime contacted you about a small project in Detroit.

If the agreement addresses staff, make sure that they can't hire away your people without your prior written consent. While you certainly can't keep someone from accepting employment elsewhere, you shouldn't expect to lose a key person to a prime. Conversely, don't expect to poach their talent either. Regarding staff, make sure their language doesn't restrict your ability to terminate someone for cause just because they are assigned to a project with the prime. If you need to terminate a staff member for theft, an agreement with a prime or client should not impact you.

In many instances, your first certification marketing experience is likely to come through your contact with supplier diversity professionals.

Chapter 18: Talking with Supplier Diversity Professionals

Dr. L. Jay Burkes, Ph.D., Comcast NBCUniversal

Dr. L. Jay Burks grew up in a family of entrepreneurs, led by women of color, so he has personally seen how certification can help remedy disparity and close the gap for diversely owned businesses. Burk began his diversity-focused career at Cheyney University (Cheyney, Pa.) working in what is now the DBE Supportive Services Center. Burks' role was to advise certified DBEs (Disadvantaged Business Enterprises) and make sure they had chances to participate in federally funded DOT projects. Burks later became director, overseeing the DBE support services and playing a pivotal role in renewing the University's grants that would help grow their client's businesses. Eventually, Burks made the leap to the State of Delaware's Office of Supplier Diversity (which is now the Division of Small Business) to impact a larger number of diverse businesses. Five years later, he joined Comcast to help an even larger group of diverse companies—Delaware's entire budget was $3 billion while Comcast's Supplier Development budget in 2018 was $4 billion.

An advocate of certification, Burks reminds us that "certification reduces marketing costs and increases competitive advantage." When a company calculates meeting its diverse spend goals "if you aren't certified, you can't be verified," so your client may look elsewhere to meet its goals. Increasing access to opportunities for diverse business is Burks' motivator, to help others be more aware of what is available to them through supplier diversity. Comcast's supplier diversity combined with its inclusion program mirrors the communities it serves. This is Comcast's foundation for innovation—one that gives diverse businesses exposure to great opportunities. As a global organization, Comcast faces the challenge of engaging with smaller diverse suppliers that may not be able to scale. Because Comcast tracks its tier two spend, Burks and the supplier diversity team strongly encourages smaller suppliers to explore opportunities to partner with a prime vendor.

Burks, like all supplier diversity representatives, gets many requests to connect with diverse suppliers. He recommends that suppliers take the time to research the company being approached. Don't lead with diversity—instead learn about the products, services and values of your targeted client as the key component of your marketing strategy before you connect. Understand that people are change resistant and that there are competing interests when you approach supplier diversity. Have a plan, don't say you can do everything, and don't make promises you are unable to keep. Finally, Burks says, "Build a relationship! Be your authentic self, and get to know the key supplier diversity and procurement people." (Burks, 2019)

Amy Criss, previously at 84 Lumber

Amy Criss grew up at 84 Lumber, beginning her career soon after graduating from California University of Pennsylvania (California, Pa.). She was eventually tasked with developing 84's MWBE program from the perspective of a large WBE. 84 Lumber, a WBENC-certified company, is comprised of nearly 250 stores, component manufacturing plants, custom door and millwork shops, and engineered wood product centers nationwide.

Criss is a tireless advocate of diverse business owners everywhere. She spends many hours helping people who will change the face of business because she believes the more connections she can help them make, the better business will become in America. Criss is passionate about diversity and helping businesses succeed, and in that the vein, she served on Governor Tom Wolfe's Advisory Council on Diversity, Inclusion, and Small Business Opportunities. This Council works collaboratively with the governor in establishing statewide goals to increase diverse business participation in state contracting opportunities. Criss was also the only non-business-owner appointed to WBENC's Forum Leadership Team. In these, and many other leadership roles, Criss successfully promotes and escalates diverse business owners locally and around the country.

She also spearheaded the Team 84 initiative, a pre-apprenticeship program for low-income residents in disadvantaged neighborhoods to gain knowledge and on–the-job training. The program utilizes large residential construction projects with MWBE requirements that 84 Lumber is contracted to help build as the training location.

Criss recommends continuous networking, not just with the large corporations and government agencies. She believes in the "opportunities to partner and do business with each other" in the diverse community: "working together benefits us all." (Criss, 2019)

Jay Sheldon Wesley, MPA, MBA, Lumen Technologies

When we caught up with Jay Sheldon Wesley in April of 2019, he was just completing his first 90 days as the new Global Corporate Supplier Diversity manager for Lumen

Technologies, the third largest telecommunications company providing communications and data services to residential, business, governmental, and wholesale customers in 37 U.S. states. Lumen procures about $11 billion in goods and services annually, and Wesley's goal is for the company to join the Billion Dollar Roundtable by 2021.

When Wesley began his career years ago, his first role was at Hughes Aircraft Company to help small, diverse businesses learn how to do business with this federal defense contractor, and it gave him a ringside seat at the evolution of supply chain and supplier diversity development, terms that didn't enter the business lexicon until the 1990s.

Wesley's mission is to help change the culture that believes supplier diversity is simply a handout to diverse vendors that are often regarded as inferior because they are new or small. He sees supplier diversity as an opportunity to level the playing field, allowing diverse businesses to compete.

When asked about building capacity, Wesley described a preference for developing suppliers rather than taking a shotgun approach. His team works to assess diverse companies in various disciplines. Once identified, he believes in helping these suppliers become ready to support his organization. That means "bid and business ready." Such assistance might involve review of bid processes or helping the supplier learn to articulate its value proposition. Wesley spoke of a transportation supplier who submitted three non-winning bids. In each instance, the supplier went through an extensive debrief to learn what was successful in the proposal and what was not. By sticking with it, the supplier won the fourth bidding opportunity, saving Wesley's then company over half a million dollars, while effectively executing the contract. Wesley's approach created a win for everyone.

For diverse business owners, Wesley recommends that we know what we sell and how it helps the company we are pitching address its pain points. He suggests we get as much cultural intelligence and cost analysis data as we can. Also, avoid fudge factors in price quotes—we shouldn't need them, and they make us less competitive. He reminds us not to sell diversity, but rather, our confidence in our world class solutions to scale and bring value to our target clients. Finally, Wesley advises we keep our own metrics on who we approach, what works, and what doesn't and work on relationship building. (Wesley, 2019)

Certify and Sell

Pathricio "Joe" McClain, Eaton

Community impact is the root of Joe McClain's engagement with diverse suppliers. Growing up in an entrepreneurial family, McClain witnessed first-hand how business can affect a community. What he learned at home has become part of his supplier diversity mission at Eaton Corporation. McClain believes that Eaton must be able to rely on its supplier diversity professionals to ensure that diverse suppliers meet Eaton's pre-qualification criteria and that the opportunities are *right-sized*, leading to successful engagements.

Eaton is unique in its scope of business. As a power management company delivering energy-efficient solutions, Eaton is not yet a BDR member, but every BDR member—28 of the world's largest procurement organizations—is an Eaton customer. McClain's challenge is not compliance, but rather ensuring that Eaton is recognized for its superior performance in supplier diversity. Eaton was named a 2018 Best of the Decade honoree for supplier diversity by Minority Business News (MBN USA), a leading minority business publication. The list was compiled based on key indicators, including:

- Impactful promotion of supplier diversity to improve a company's business performance

- Identification of strategic opportunities to include and grow diverse suppliers
- Creation of a positive environment for procurement employees
- Encouragement of innovative ideas among employees and suppliers

One innovative idea is Eaton's survey of its supplier base to quantify the economic impact of its diverse suppliers. The study looks at revenues, employment numbers, volunteerism, and charitable contributions as a way to measure how its supplier diversity program affects communities around the world.

Eaton is a member of Disability:IN, NaVOBA, NGLCC, NMSDC, WBENC, and WeConnect. Eaton's support of employee resource groups (ERG) bolsters supplier diversity's mission. When Eaton comes to a national diversity business conference, it comes with ERG leaders and members prepared to engage with and inform conference attendees on doing business with Eaton.

McClain says diverse suppliers need to be prepared, which is different than being ready, when it comes to engaging with supplier diversity. Being prepared means you don't walk in and ask "What does Eaton do?" He says that is the most deflating question a supplier can ask and demonstrates that they have not even bothered to visit the corporate website. He recommends that you do the research and come prepared to offer solutions. And, never, ever reply "whatever you want" when asked what you can do for them. (McClain, 2019)

Fernando Hernandez, Microsoft

Fernando Hernandez became involved with sustainability and diversity in 2005. As Microsoft's Director of Supplier Diversity & Sustainability, Hernandez believes this is the only business area where progress and diversity are of mutual self-interest. In search of the next billion customers globally, it is good business sense to work with vendors reflective of their customers' culture.

Challenges at a company like Microsoft involve staying relevant, concurrently, in multiple disciplines across all the product and service lines. To do that, purchased products must meet Microsoft's sustainability goals. This is where we begin to understand the huge scope and breadth of issues facing sustainability and diversity. When looking at diverse suppliers, Hernandez is interested in their insight into the technology areas that will impact the sales cycle in both the short and long term. He recommends that suppliers not sell on the past, be self-aware, and try not to sell old or outdated technology. They should position to lead into the future with technology for the companies that are turning science fiction into science fact.

Microsoft's supplier diversity database has over 14,000 vendors listed, with about 800 of them currently providing goods and services. Hernandez recommends that suppliers keep their records up to date, because their first stop is to engage directly with vendors in that database. If adequate resources aren't available in the database, the next step is to talk with NMSDC and WBENC about new members who might be appropriate. Supplier diversity professionals are a tight-knit group, and Hernandez gets and shares referrals within this community. (Hernandez, 2020)

Heather Herndon Wright, Director of Supply Chain Diversity for Vistra Energy

Heather Herndon Wright is a wealth of information, because she has seen supplier diversity from just about every angle. First, working with the Dallas Fort Worth (DFW) Airport Board as a minority business development liaison, she learned about the remedial nature of systemic disadvantages experienced by diverse business owners. Wright, a Native American, had early involvement with NMSDC. (Later, she

served with the National Association of Women Business
Owners [NAWBO] to develop a certification program offered
to MBEs, VBEs, and WBEs. And, she currently serves on the
board of NaVOBA.) Eventually, though, it became apparent
that WBEs needed a national certification program of their
own, and Wright became actively involved with WBENC. Since
then, she's been a WBE business owner and is currently
Director of Supply Chain Diversity for Vistra Energy.

Wright was there when NMSDC returned to its roots of
certifying only ethnic minorities; by default, white women
business owners had nowhere to go, as mentioned in Chapter
14. She says, typically, these were businesses that might be the
most likely pressured to be fronts since they tended to be
married to white males. There was not only a need to certify
and support WBEs, but also a real need to vet or verify that the
businesses were legitimate WBEs. The Dallas Fort Worth
(DFW) Minority Supplier Diversity Council decided to create a
new division to specifically certify women businesses based on
gender. They selected Wright to help lead the effort,
establishing what is now known as Women's Business Council
Southwest.

The plan was to grandmother in the 193 WBEs
disenfranchised by NMSDC. In an interesting twist, one of the

first applicant companies was initially denied certification by the Women's Business Council because it had three owners—33% Hispanic American male, 33% African American male, and 34% Caucasian American female. This company did not meet the criteria for a gender-based certification.

A few years later, Wright joined Fujitsu to create a supplier diversity initiative there. When Fujitsu became a board member of the DFW Minority Supplier Diversity Council where Wright had once been staff, she became secretary of the board. Eventually, Wright established a women's enterprise magazine and a consulting company, both also certified MWBE businesses, before venturing back into the corporate world with Vistra where she remains deeply connected to the third-party certifiers.

In supplier diversity, Wright sees a major challenge in the "perception that maybe we don't need supplier diversity any more, that we've got this inclusivity down" at executive levels. Supplier diversity clout seems to be diminishing. Exacerbated by a lack of succession planning, as the original generation of professionals retire, people aren't being promoted into executive levels (e.g. VP or Chief Diversity Officer) that demonstrate the importance or impact of supplier diversity in corporations. As diverse suppliers and business owners become investors, Wright believes that increased supplier diversity reporting will raise visibility once again. (Wright, Vistra Director, Supply Chain Diversity, 2020)

Chapter 19: Capacity Building

Certification helps get you in the conversation, but often, the question of a business's ability to perform is what prevents a sale. Newly certified companies and new businesses are frequently advised by supplier diversity representatives that they need to build capacity. Many of them then turn to people like us, asking "What does that mean?" Capacity building is how you build your organization and its ability to take on larger projects or sales. You can build capacity by incrementally increasing sales, building your infrastructure (adding equipment or technology), or increasing staff expertise through education and training.

John Scifers' experience, described above, is a perfect example of a corporation helping build capacity. Mr. Richards' guidance and mentorship helped Scifers build not one, but two successful SDVOSB companies. Amy Criss at 84 Lumber freely introduces minority- and women-owned businesses to buyers, personal introductions that give these owners access to opportunities not otherwise available. Jay Wesley has been an ardent advisor to diverse business in how to prepare to compete and win business at every stop in his career. We celebrate these jewels! But, there is still work to be done.

Certify and Sell

Government agencies and corporations see inherit risk in awarding projects—particularly large ones—to a small business, no matter how long they've been in business because of the capacity issue. They're relying on you to meet a business need, one that could very well effect how their customers perceive them and their bottom line. Our company was very lucky to have its first contract with Westinghouse Electric Corporation, but our founder had chased and won contracts with them in the past when employed by other companies. The only reason one of their buyers took a risk on a fledgling start-up in 1983 was that she had delivered in the past and was expected to continue to do so.

Smaller projects, performing as a sub-contractor, etc. are ways for businesses to prove their capability and build out their capacity with commercial and government clients. This is a realistic approach, but the type of business you operate will determine if such contracts are available. For example, our industry has changed drastically in the 37 years we've been in business. Remember, our first contract was with one of the largest U.S. corporations at the time, and we used to be a direct supplier to many Fortune 100 companies, including IBM, Purina Mills, and Bayer. But, along with the growth of supplier diversity came the birth of supply chains and the metrics of procurement.

These large companies determined that it is more cost-effective to work with one or two large vendors of our services and made it necessary for us to sub-contract. In some cases, that worked. In others, it became financially untenable, and we lost decades-old relationships because the intermediary (master service provider) was mandated to control costs, reducing the prices they were willing to pay. Our industry was basically turned into a commodity. And, commodities compete primarily on price. New businesses will eventually be subject to their own disruptions ... because nothing ever stays the same, except change.

That change is what drove us to find a new marketplace for our service offerings: government. And, not the federal government. Our sweet spot has been state governments. We always recommend that business owners take a look at local- and state-level government customers because they buy such a vast array of goods and services.

How Corporations and Government Can Help

As the data becomes better, organizations should be able to use it to evaluate disparity and the availability of diverse suppliers when setting their goals. We frequently hear remarks about the disconnect between supplier diversity and their purchasing or procurement departments in many large companies. We believe the reason government agencies are experiencing better diverse participation may be due to the legislation or executive orders that *require them to meet diverse goals.* If businesses *mandate and articulate* supplier diversity goals across the breadth of their procurement chain, those goals are more likely to become reality. Our supplier diversity plan is pretty simple. And, everyone in the company that has any purchasing authority knows what the rules are. That is not always the case in larger organizations, but it would be a great goal.

Companies could review their procurement data from the last ten years and compare their actual providers vs. the pool of available diverse providers. This kind of review might show that there have been no changes in providers for a specific good or service, compared to an increased number of potential providers listed in supplier diversity. A good test might be to develop a request for a quote or proposal that either requires diverse participation or results in multiple awards amongst prior and new suppliers.

Companies might want to review master service provider (MSP) agreements to determine if they are truly cost effective and/or whether these programs help build diverse business capacity. For example, there was a big push in our industry to streamline procurement through a few MSPs, reducing overhead. It also fostered a reduction in billing and compensation rates, making a human-based resource into a commodity-like sales model. In one instance that we know of, a large customer required us to provide a consultant through a preferred MSP. The preferred MSP specified our billing rate, invoiced the client and paid us. We discovered, retroactively, that the end client's charges were 40% higher than if they dealt with us directly[21].

Smaller contract bundles might be an excellent approach, particularly where agencies can identify a specific scope of work in larger procurements that can be purchased separately. Some states give their agencies the power to procure, without the onerous formal request for proposal (RFP) process. It is often based on smaller-dollar volume purchases. The contracting officer might be able to buy using cash, government purchase cards, purchase orders (PO), and blanket purchase agreements. The businesses interested in winning these government contracts and bids can simply

---

[21] One wonders about MSPs and the definition of a pass-through, but commercially useful functions and pass-through terminology only appear to apply to government contracting.

submit a quote, with a contract resulting once a quote is accepted and an order is placed by the agency. Each state is different, and laws change but here are some examples as of January 2020:

- Arkansas small order method is used for purchases up to $20,000, or up to $40,000 if purchased from a certified MBE or WBE.

- California allows purchases under $5,000 dollars. Agencies can issue contracts to certified small or micro-businesses or service-disabled veteran-owned businesses (SDVOB) when the contract value is greater than $5,000 but less than $250,000 and the agency has received quotes from two small or micro-business or two SDVOBs.

- Idaho exempts contracts under $25,000.

- South Carolina's "Director of the Division of Procurement Services may authorize an individual governmental body to make direct procurements not under term contracts in an amount up to one hundred fifty thousand dollars. All authority granted pursuant to this item must be in writing, and the director shall advise the board in writing of all such authorizations."

What do Organizations Buy?

What follows is a list of example products and services that different organizations may buy. It is by no means comprehensive.

Cities/Counties: paper, phone systems, placement services, event planning, catering, signage, janitorial services, park maintenance (grass cutting), signaling equipment (stop signs, traffic lights, etc.), playground equipment, temporary staffing, toilet paper, vehicles (cars, vans, trucks), park equipment, bottled water, first responder materials (training, counselling, vehicles, sirens, radios), insurance, assessment services, legal services, newspapers.

Retail Outlets: credit card processing, all the products they sell to consumers or businesses. *What products does Walmart sell? Who provides them with those products? Who delivers those products to the stores?* Talk about a huge supply chain, A to Z: Aspirin, baby clothes, cat food, DVDs, Elmer's glue, futons, garbage bags, hammers, ice, jelly and jam, kites, lamps, mustard, nail polish, olive oil, Parcheesi, Q-tips, rice, swing sets, tires, underwear, vacuum cleaners, windshield wipers, Xbox controllers, yogurt, and zip ties!

Departments of Transportation (City/County/State/ Federal): architectural services, fencing, flagging, hauling, cement, asphalt, signage, engineering services, porta potties, bridge building, tunnel maintenance, guard rails, culverts, signaling (traffic lights), lighting, mowing, road treatments (salt, cinders), snow removal, traffic cones. *DOT includes airport authorities, local and regional transit authorities, and thruway/turnpike authorities that buy* vehicles, busses, rail cars, gasoline, CNG fuel, aviation gas, waiting room furnishings, scales, baggage handling, signage (stop, road signs), EZ Pass systems, coin sorters.

Manufacturing Companies: raw materials, tools, temporary staffing or placement services, inspection services, equipment (computers, assembly lines, fans, fork lifts, dust collectors), apparel (uniforms), safety gear (acoustic protection, hard hats, filtration masks, gloves), cafeteria furnishings, vending machine services.

Hospitals: food, nutritional supplements, vitamins, medications, clothing, laundry services, gloves, sanitary items, patient kits (toothbrushes, toothpastes, shampoo, body wash), Purell, network services, telephone services and equipment, lighting, durable medical goods (crutches, walkers, wheel chairs), trays, silverware, landscaping, snow removal, janitorial supplies, surgical instruments, Band-Aids, Kleenex, dishes, pitchers, glasses, trash bags, patient gowns, x-ray film, cafeteria furnishings, vending services.

Facilities Management (Private or Government Buildings): furniture, lighting (indoor and outdoor), interior design and/or decoration, plants, janitorial services, grounds keeping services (planting, trimming, mowing, snow removal), elevator/escalator repair, window washing, security services, restroom supplies, window coverings, floor coverings (carpeting, vinyl, wood), art (e.g. paintings, sculptures, photographs), building supplies, paint, phone/Internet services, printing/mailing services, insurance, legal services.

Development Companies/Housing Authorities: property (title searches, financing), architectural services, legal services (contracts), and general contractors (for construction). *General contractors generally engage electricians, plumbers, drywall, carpentry, brick/stone masonry, and painting subcontractors.* Each specialty has its own building supplies and tools to purchase. GCs or architects specify windows, skylights, sinks, toilets, appliances, and wall and floor coverings, which must be purchased and installed.

Colleges/Universities: food/cafeteria services, guest speakers, athletics (equipment, field/pool maintenance, trophies, banners, flags), ATMs, dorm furnishings, historical preservation, laboratory equipment, chemicals, art supplies, theater (costumes, music, makeup, curtains, props, a/v, microphones), religious supplies (rosaries, pastor services), awards, diplomas, printing services (embossing, engraving, embroidery), mailing services, agricultural supplies (animals, feed, vets, seed, fertilizer), skylights; solar panels, backup generators, classroom furnishings (desks, black boards, cork boards, projectors, chalk), conference facilities, medical supplies (surgical equipment, cadavers, beakers, pharmaceuticals, etc.), advertising/marketing.

Hotels/Resorts: credit card processing, toiletries (shampoo, conditioner, soaps, body lotion, shoe polisher), bedding (sheets, towels, pillows, blankets, mattresses.), ice machines, laundry supplies or services, trash bags, art/décor, furnishings (chairs, desks, dressers, lamps, mirrors), spa supplies (robes, oils, scents), batteries (hundreds of remotes and fire alarms), Bibles/Books of Mormon, curtains/draperies, floral arrangements, mailing supplies (stamps/stationery, notepads, pens), elevator maintenance, luggage carts, phone systems, breakfast buffet supplies, in-room coffee/tea supplies, casino supplies (dice, cards, chips), alarm systems, fire suppressant systems, flatware, carts, glasses, mini-fridges.

County/State/Federal Prisons: food, nutritional supplements, vitamins, medications, clothing, laundry services, barber services/hair dresser services, fencing, safety equipment, ammunition, health services, pastoral services, uniforms, jail management systems, periodicals, concessions, mail services, gym/sports equipment, underwear, socks, soap and shampoo, printing services, counselling services, paper, internet/phone services.

Entertainment Venues/TV Stations: cameras, lighting (studio and office), office equipment, TV sets, computers and fax machines, microphones, office supplies, insurance, mix boards, makeup, wardrobe, sound technicians, office furniture, vending machines, helicopters (own or lease, maintenance), production support, props, costumes, wrist bands, tickets, trash cans, parking lot maintenance (line painting, repaving), insurance, production studios and booths, blue screens, fleet maintenance and fuel, concessions, janitorial services, temporary staffing.

Insurance Companies: paper, printing services, actuarial services, postage and shipping services, auditing services, records management (storage, destruction), independent sales agents, forms, envelopes, investigative services, computers, phone/Internet services, privacy protection, legal services, office furnishings, fax machines, travel services, advertising and branded trinkets.

Other Requests

We have seen notifications from various cities, boroughs, counties, and states for all kinds of goods and services. These are a few examples.

- Auction services
- Psychological support services for law enforcement personnel
- Shredding services for city and city schools
- Closed caption television (CCTV) inspections web viewer specifications
- Community or sampling surveys
- Professional services: certified public accounting firm
- Branding, media, and experiential marketing services
- Strategic coaching for public schools
- Compensation studies, HR task/resource analysis, or employee benefit and communications consulting services

- Conservation work to be performed on circuit court records
- Automated vehicle location system for school buses and other vehicles
- Evaluation of a police department's use of force data
- Review and update of the historic district guidelines
- Central signal system (CSS) solution for the signalized intersections
- Professional engineering and design services for harbor and river deepening projects in compliance with the Army Corps of Engineers' criteria.
- Procurement disparity study – *disparity studies are contracts themselves!*
- Art therapy for older adults
- Consulting services for Ryan White Part B HIV/AIDS Program
- Cyber security vulnerability assessment
- K–5 reading (English language) core textbooks and ancillary materials
- Education training and support services
- Team nutrition training and workshops
- Appraisal services
- Environmental land surveys

Certify and Sell

- Redevelopment housing authority professional legal services
- Jail management system, inmate telephone system, inmate commissary services component, inmate trust accounting software component, kiosk network component, staff/inmate handheld electronic devices component, and inmate email system
- Comprehensive organizational and operational transformations consulting
- Professional services for transportation planning
- Professional services construction-engineering-inspection
- Updating the town's SCADA system with new supervisory system software and hardware
- Fire policy manual and daily training bulletins
- Licensed architectural/engineering firms to assist in the development of plans and specifications for construction of a Prototype II, Class B burn building
- Telecomm and cable strategy consulting support
- Professional electrical engineering services
- Provide state advocacy services to the City of Chesapeake and Chesapeake Schools
- Workers' compensation claims and cost containment services

- Provide professional mechanical, electrical, and plumbing engineering and consulting services
- Provide professional civil sanitary services
- Data analytics for instructional improvement
- Body removal services
- Law enforcement/public safety incident-based reporting system (IBR), records management system, and computer aided dispatch system to include mobile data terminals (MDTs)
- Design and deliver a customized customer service social skills training program for transportation and maintenance employees
- Trauma registry
- Professional services to support renegotiation of the City's cable franchise agreement

What Can Diverse Businesses Do?

Growth Walk

Walking the walk is critical for diverse businesses. We expect large corporations and government agencies to help us along the way, so we should be willing to put our efforts and money where our mouths are.

- Do you need subcontractors to help you fulfill a contract? Find potential diverse team members through your certifiers and the state MWBE offices.
- Do you need a caterer? Certified ones work near you. Check with your certifier.
- Do you need help with marketing, book keeping, office cleaning, or transportation? Certifiers have lists of certified companies that will be happy to hear from you.

Network with, train, and mentor the new small and micro businesses in your area. Help them understand the power of certification. Engage with them when you have any opportunity to share your stories, and guide those who would like to avoid some of the pitfalls we've all encountered.

Succession Plans

What happens when a certified company is no longer certifiable? This can happen for several reasons. Perhaps the owner became so successful they were able to sell the business. Remember that diversity certification eligibility is co-dependent. Ownership changes, certification expires. When you begin working on your exit plan, you could specify sale to another diverse owner(s), perhaps even one you have been grooming to take over the business. Helping the new owner qualify and apply for continued certification will not only leave your business in good hands but help your clients retain the diversity spend that they count on with you.

Chapter 20: International Certifiers

Do your customers play globally? If you look at the Billion Dollar Round Table members, the answer is definitely yes. If you can support them globally, an international certification could be another marketing tool for your business. Many international supplier diversity programs, processes, and policies have been established based on the models NMSDC and WBENC developed in the United States.

Global Supplier Diversity Alliance

This organization provides a unique collaborative and effective global supplier diversity platform representing international supplier diversity advocacy organizations in five countries. The following five partners are recognized by NMSDC's as their **Global-Link International Program**.

Australia: Supply Nation

Founded in 2009, Supply Nation works with Aboriginal and Torres Strait Islander businesses along with procurement teams from within Australia's government and corporate sectors to help grow the Indigenous business sector. Supply Nation recognizes two levels of Indigenous ownership—

Registered Suppliers (>50% Indigenous ownership) and Certified Suppliers (>51% Indigenous-owned, managed, and controlled). Supply Nation's five-step verification process ensures that all businesses listed on Indigenous Business Direct (Supply Nation's directory), are not only Indigenous-owned but are also regularly audited for changes in company structure and ownership.

Canada: CAMSC

The Canadian Aboriginal and Minority Supplier Council (CAMSC) was established in 2004. A CAMSC certified supplier is a business owned, managed, and controlled (>51%) by Aboriginal peoples or visible minorities. According to the Government of Canada, visible minorities are defined as persons nonwhite in color and non-Caucasian in race. Visible minority classifications include Chinese, South Asian, Black, West Asian, Filipino, South East Asian, Latin American, Japanese, and Korean. According to the Government of Canada, Aboriginal peoples include First Nations, Metis, and Inuit.

China: MSDChina

Minority Supplier Development in China (MSDChina) was initiated and established in 2008 as the first national nonprofit platform in China dedicated to driving the development of China's minority-owned businesses by connecting minority suppliers with purchasing corporations for procurement opportunities on a mutually beneficial basis. MSDChina establishes a platform for communications and business exchanges between minority suppliers and purchasing corporations and develops the minority suppliers into competitive and successful regional and global suppliers.

South Africa: SASDC

The South African Supplier Diversity Council (SASDC) was founded in January 2011 and operates as a nonprofit company with members in terms of the Companies Act, 71 of 2008 of the Republic of South Africa. It is an independent not-for-profit entity, controlled by its corporate members, under the direction of a majority corporate-member-nominated board of directors. The purpose of the SASDC is to:

- Promote business and commerce through transformation.
- Serve as a conduit for corporate South Africa to reach black-owned enterprises that are able to provide them with products and services, recognizing such qualifying black enterprises as beneficiaries of the Company.

- Act as the intersection for corporate members and a growing pool of black-owned enterprises to engage in sustainable business linkages through efficient targeted procurement programs and effective enterprise and supplier development practices. In so doing, it contributes to political and economic stability and enhances the country's economic competitiveness as a key to sustained growth.

United Kingdom: MSDUK

Minority Supplier and Diversity UK was founded in 2006. Minority business is defined as for-profit enterprise, of any size, physically located in the United Kingdom, and majority (51% or more) owned, managed, and controlled by people of ethnic minority origin, provided such individual/individuals are British Nationals and/or permanent residents with indefinite leave to remain in the UK.

US-based businesses certified by NMSDC can follow the instructions of each organization to seek reciprocal status with them and gain access to their networks.

WEConnect International

Affiliated with WBENC, this is a global network that connects women-owned businesses to qualified buyers around the world. WEConnect International identifies, educates, registers, and certifies women's business enterprises based outside of the U.S. that are at least 51% owned, as well as managed and controlled, by one or more women and then connects them with multinational corporate buyers. WEConnect includes:

- Africa: Nigeria, South Africa
- Asia: Bangladesh, Greater China, India, Indonesia, Japan, Malaysia, Singapore
- Australasia
- Europe: Germany, The Netherlands, Switzerland, Turkey, UK, and Ireland
- Latin America
- Middle East, North Africa
- North America: Canada, United States

US-based businesses certified by WBENC can register with WEConnect International, gaining access to their network, by submitting a shortened application (that includes providing a copy of their WBENC certificate) and paying their $500 USD fee.

Like its counterparts, the NGLCC and Disability:IN have global initiatives.

NGLCC Global

Comprised of chambers and business networks, the National Gay and Lesbian Chamber of Commerce (NGLCC) Global was established to promote "economic empowerment as well as inclusive economic growth for LGBTI[22] people and LGBTI-owned businesses." NGLCC Global includes:

- Australia: Gay and Lesbian Organization of Business and Enterprise (GLOBE)
- Brazil: Câmara de Comércio Lésbica, Gay, Bisexual, e Transgênera Brasileira (CCLGBTB)
- Canada: Canadian Gay and Lesbian Chamber of Commerce (CGLCC)
- Central & Eastern Europe: East Meets West
- Colombia: Cámara de Comerciantes LGBT de Colombia (CCLGBTco)

---

[22] LGBTI = Lesbian, Gay, Bisexual, Transgender, and Intersex

- Costa Rica: Cámara de Comercio Diversa Costa Rica (CCDCR)
- Dominican Republic: Cámara de Comercio LGBT de la República Dominicana (CCLGBTRD)
- India: RWS—India's Diverse Chamber of Commerce
- Italy: Italian GLBT Business Chamber
- Jamaica: Jamaican Association of Diverse Businesses
- Mexico: Federación Mexicana de Empresarios LGBT (FME-LGBT)
- Scandinavia: Scandinavian Gay and Lesbian Chamber of Commerce (SGLCC)
- South Africa: PLUS
- Uruguay: Cámara de Comercio & Negocios LGBT de Uruguay (CCNLGBTU)

Gay and Lesbian Organization of Business and Enterprise (GLOBE)

GLOBE was founded in 1992 to aid LGBTIQ+ communities, small businesses, and professionals; within six months it established connections across Victoria and around Australia. Its mission is to "provide opportunities to network and grow in a professional, safe and inclusive environment that empowers, supports and enables our communities to achieve their full potential."

Canadian Gay and Lesbian Chamber of Commerce (CGLCC)

Established in 2003, CGLCC's mission is to assist LGBT+ businesses with access, engagement, visibility, and support, fostering economic growth for them in the wider business community.

East Meets West

Established in Vienna, Austria, in 2013, East Meets West now services the following countries through their network: Albania, Austria, Bosnia, Bulgaria, Croatia, Czech Republic, Hungary, Kosovo, Macedonia, Poland, Romania, Russia, Serbia, Slovakia, Slovenia, and Ukraine. They've played a role in introducing the concept of supplier diversity in these countries and they provide services to their members such as business feasibility checks, connection to finance, and a depository of business examples. In 2018, it joined with SGLCC and IGLBT to form the European LGBTI Chamber of Commerce.

Certify and Sell

Cámara de Comerciantes LGBT de Colombia (CCLGBTco)

Established in 2012 CCLBTco's imitative is to economically and socially strengthen Colombia's LGBTI community—companies, independent professionals, and other LGBT organizations.

Cámara de Comercio Diversa Costa Rica (CCDCR)

Established in 2015 CCDCR advocates for, promotes, and works to strengthen LGTBQ businesses in Costa Rica.

RWS (Rajmala Welfare Society)

Serves as India's Diverse Chamber of Commerce, founded to "empower the LGBTQIA community of India and provide them equal opportunities as part of the mainstream."

Italian GLBT Business Chamber

Founded in 2017 IGLBT is a "networking business platform to facilitate and promote the growth of Italian LGBT enterprises through the creation of new commercial relations with other LGBT enterprises as well with bigger corporations, in Italy and abroad." In 2018, it joined with SGLCC and East Meets West to form the European LGBTI Chamber of Commerce.

Jamaican Association of Diverse Businesses

The Jamaican Association of Diverse Businesses is a network of businesses and professionals committed to economic growth and development of the Jamaican LGBT business community.

Federación Mexicana de Empresarios LGBT (FME-LGBT)

Founded in 2014, FMELGBT works "for the economic empowerment of our sector through the linking of LGBT+ suppliers, multinational corporations, government entities, and civil society organizations to generate business opportunities, promote norms, policies and regulations in favor of inclusion and diversity in the economic and labor field."

Scandinavian Gay and Lesbian Chamber of Commerce (SGLCC)

Working in Sweden (through their affiliate, AmCham Sweden) and Scandinavia, SGLCC connects the corporate sector with LGBT businesses community. In 2018 it joined with IGLBT and East Meets West to form the European LGBTI Chamber of Commerce.

Certify and Sell

PLUS

Established in 2016, PLUS "champions, promotes, supports and empowers South African lesbian, gay, bisexual, transgender, and intersex [LGBTI] business owners and entrepreneurs."

Cámara de Comercio & Negocios LGBT de Uruguay (CCNLGBTU)

Founded in 2015, the mission of CCNLGBTU is to "strengthen the business and competitiveness of Uruguayan companies committed to diversity, promoting networking and internationalization of their products and services, while providing business tools for the economic and social development of the LGBT community in Uruguay."

United States-based businesses certified by NGLCC can register as an International LGBTI Supplier through the My.NGLCC portal.

Disability:IN's Global Directory

Disability:IN's Global Directory is "a collaborative disability inclusion database with country profiles to help companies achieve disability inclusion and equality around the world." Information provided for each country listed includes

206

disability definition, legislation, employer legal requirements, accessibility requirements, cultural norms, business practices/examples, insights, supplier diversity, talent sourcing resources, additional resources, and references. Countries include—

- Argentina
  https://private.disabilityin.org/global/argentina/
- Australia
  https://private.disabilityin.org/global/australia/
- Belgium
  https://private.disabilityin.org/global/belgium/
- Brazil https://private.disabilityin.org/global/brazil/
- Canada https://private.disabilityin.org/global/canada/
- Chile https://private.disabilityin.org/global/chile/
- China https://private.disabilityin.org/global/china/
- Colombia
  https://private.disabilityin.org/global/colombia/
- Costa Rica
  https://private.disabilityin.org/global/costa-rica/
- Ecuador
  https://private.disabilityin.org/global/ecuador/
- Egypt https://private.disabilityin.org/global/egypt/
- France https://private.disabilityin.org/global/france/

- Germany
  https://private.disabilityin.org/global/germany/
- Hong Kong
  https://private.disabilityin.org/global/hongkong/
- India https://private.disabilityin.org/global/india
- Ireland https://private.disabilityin.org/global/ireland
- Israel https://private.disabilityin.org/global/israel
- Italy https://private.disabilityin.org/global/italy
- Japan https://private.disabilityin.org/global/japan
- Mexico https://private.disabilityin.org/global/mexico
- The Netherlands
  https://private.disabilityin.org/global/the-netherlands
- The Philippines
  https://private.disabilityin.org/global/the-philippines
- Russian Federation
  https://private.disabilityin.org/global/russian-
  federation
- Singapore
  https://private.disabilityin.org/global/singapore
- South Africa
  https://private.disabilityin.org/global/south-africa
- Spain https://private.disabilityin.org/global/spain
- Switzerland
  https://private.disabilityin.org/global/switzerland

- Taiwan https://private.disabilityin.org/global/taiwan
- United Kingdom
  https://private.disabilityin.org/global/united-kingdom
- United States
  https://private.disabilityin.org/global/united-states

Chapter 21: 2020 Impacts on Supplier Diversity and DEI

When we talked with Heather Herndon Wright in Chapter 18, she expressed concerns about the "perception that maybe we don't need supplier diversity any more, that we've got this inclusivity down" (Wright, Vistra Director, Supply Chain Diversity, 2020). That conversation took place before COVID-19 and the unfathomable public murder of George Floyd in May of 2020. These two events have altered the conscious awareness of all Americans and exposed documented reasons for Wright's concerns.

George Floyd/Black Lives Matter

While there have been many news stories, articles and autopsy reports claiming additional mitigating factors in Floyd's death, the single video speaks volumes. Perhaps it is insensitive to say that we don't care about Floyd's background, theoretical drug use, or if he paid for his cigarettes with a counterfeit $20 bill (would you recognize one in your change?). So be it. No one deserves the treatment Floyd received. That the video exists and has been viewed so often has ignited a furious flurry of activity. "As with numerous other police-involved deaths, peaceful protests for racial justice took place to call attention to this ongoing concern. Black Lives Matter and other activists behind the protests have issued numerous complaints against police for racial discrimination and brutality in policing communities of color. They have also demanded investment in Black, Indigenous and People of Color (BIPOC) communities and disinvestment in police services." (Gulliver-Garcia, 2020) Donations to anti-racism organizations are examples of corporate activism by organizations like:

- A pledge of $400 million over five years to "to lift up Black communities and increase Black representation at PepsiCo."
- PayPal will invest $530 million to advance racial equity and inclusion.
- Apple committed $100 million to new racial equity and justice initiatives.
- Gingko Bioworks is committing $1 million "towards building a more equitable company, technology, and society."
- Bank of America is getting to the root of systemic racism with a pledge of $1 billion over four years "to help local communities address economic and racial inequality accelerated by a global pandemic."

- LEGO is donating $4 million to organizations in the United States that support black children and educate children about racial equality. They also introduced a line of braille-marked building blocks during the summer of 2020.
- Cisco pledged $5 million to charities dedicated to fighting racism and discrimination.
- The HP Foundation will donate $500,000 to social justice organizations and double-match employee contributions.
- Uber Technologies announced it will donate a total of $1 million to two criminal justice reform organizations: the Center for Policing Equity and the Equal Justice Initiative.
- Verizon Communications has committed $10 million to seven social justice organizations: the National Urban League, the National Association for the Advancement of Colored People (NAACP), National Action Network, Leadership Conference for Civil and Human Rights, Rainbow Push Coalition, National Coalition on Black Civic Participation, and NAACP Legal Defense and Educational Fund.

We believe this list will continue to grow exponentially (Sault, 2020), as will the movement's effect on corporate branding choices—both Aunt Jemima and the Washington Redskins announced planned changes to names and/or logos in 2020 as well.

COVID-19 Pandemic

Not to downplay the importance of racial justice, but when COVID-19 rolled around, it exposed many reasons for concern. One can use so many perspectives to look at unintended consequences and the true intersectionality of this pandemic.

Essential workers start with our heroic healthcare workers who have been in the thick of treating COVID patients in often dangerous conditions (insufficient personal protective equipment) and with too few resources, with a lack of relief. In April 2020, 27 COVID-19-related health worker deaths were estimated to have occurred in the USA, 106 in the UK, and 180 in Russia, with tens of thousands of infections. Beyond healthcare, millions of workers have jobs that are considered essential: custodial staff and orderlies in hospitals, teachers, childcare workers, grocery clerks and supermarket workers, delivery people, factory and farm workers, and restaurant staff. "What constitutes an essential worker in the USA varies by state, but black and Latino Americans make up a large part of the essential workforce and have been disproportionately affected by COVID-19.

Certify and Sell

In New York City, over 60% of COVID-19 deaths have been in black and Latinx populations. 120 employees of the Metropolitan Transportation Authority (MTA) died due to COVID-19, and nearly 400 have tested positive. (Collection, 2020) BIPOC are more likely to be uninsured than non-Hispanic whites. Healthcare access may also be limited for members of this group by other issues: transportation, child care, ability to take time off of work; communication and language barriers; cultural differences between patients and providers; and historical and current discrimination in healthcare systems. Some may hesitate to seek care because they distrust the government and healthcare systems responsible for inequities in treatment and historical events such as the theft of Henrietta Lacks cells, Tuskegee Study of Untreated Syphilis in the African American Male, and sterilization without people's permission. (Corona Virus-19, 2020)

COVID-19 CASES, HOSPITALIZATION, AND DEATH BY RACE/ETHNICITY

FACTORS THAT INCREASE COMMUNITY SPREAD AND INDIVIDUAL RISK	CROWDED SITUATIONS	CLOSE / PHYSICAL CONTACT	ENCLOSED SPACE	DURATION OF EXPOSURE

Rate ratios compared to White, Non-Hispanic Persons	American Indian or Alaska Native, Non-Hispanic persons	Asian, Non-Hispanic persons	Black or African American, Non-Hispanic persons	Hispanic or Latino persons
CASES[1]	2.8x higher	1.1x higher	2.6x higher	2.8x higher
HOSPITALIZATION[2]	5.3x higher	1.3x higher	4.7x higher	4.6x higher
DEATH[3]	1.4x higher	No Increase	2.1x higher	1.1x higher

Race and ethnicity are risk markers for other underlying conditions that impact health — including socioeconomic status, access to health care, and increased exposure to the virus due to occupation (e.g., frontline, essential, and critical infrastructure workers).

ACTIONS TO REDUCE RISK OF COVID-19	WEARING A MASK	SOCIAL DISTANCING (6 FT GOAL)	HAND HYGIENE	CLEANING AND DISINFECTION

CDC

[1] Data source: COVID-19 case-level data reported by state and territorial jurisdictions. Case-level data include about 95% of total reported cases. Numbers are unadjusted rate ratios.

[2] Data source: COVID-NET (https://www.cdc.gov/coronavirus/2019-ncov/covid-data/covidnet/index.html, accessed 08/06/20). Numbers are ratios of age-adjusted rates.

[3] Data source: NCHS Provisional Death Counts (https://www.cdc.gov/nchs/nvss/vsrr/COVID19/index.htm, accessed 08/06/20). Numbers are unadjusted rate ratios.

cdc.gov/coronavirus

CS314366-A 08/06/2020

Report as of 8/18/2020

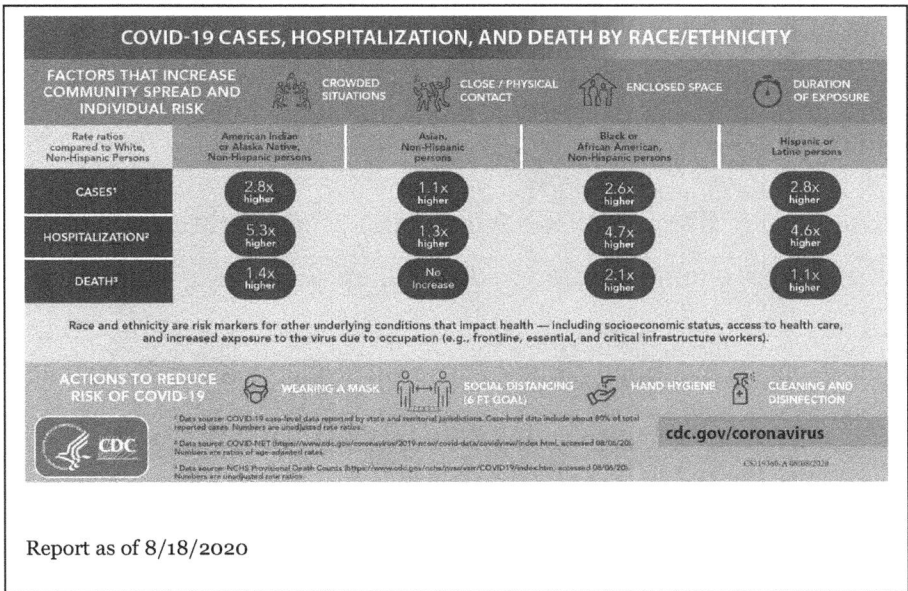

One in five Americans lives with a disability. It is the largest group of "othered" in the US. Disability doesn't respect race, gender, age, religion, sexual orientation or country of origin— it is truly equal opportunity.

It seems that people with intellectual disabilities and autism who contract COVID-19 may die at higher rates than the rest of the population. And, because they often live in congregant housing, they also contract the virus at a higher rate, according to an NPR study. Information collected in Pennsylvania shows this group is dying at a rate twice as high as other

215

Pennsylvanians. And, in New York, arguably suffering the most COVID-19 related deaths, data shows people with developmental disabilities die at a rate 2.5 times the rate of others. (Shapiro, 2020)

People who live with disabilities may encounter new or exacerbated challenges for in home health care or assistance and adapting to the recommended hand-washing regimes. Our aunt Marjorie, who passed away before the ADA was enacted in 1990, would be one of those highly challenged. Completely paralyzed by rheumatoid arthritis, she required home health aides 23 out of 24 hours and was physically incapable of washing her own hands. Others will encounter different barriers.

- Communication: getting information might be more difficult for people with vision, hearing, and even cognitive disabilities, and you can't lip read through a mask. Strategic: social distancing is impossible for those who require attendant care or reside in assisted living facilities.
- Access to care: allocation of medical resources may be discriminatory against patients with disabilities, and complaints have been filed in multiple states about these rationing policies. (Swenor, 2020)

2020 in the Diversity and Inclusion (D&I) Community

While the discussion of George Floyd and COVID-19 may seem irrelevant to the overarching diversity certification topic of this book, none of us can operate in a vacuum. The groups most affected are those whose members seek certification, and many of the persons working in D&I are members of these communities, as well. In January 2020, people predicting the top D&I topics for this year had no clue about what was to transpire. Most seem to agree that D&I would become DEI or Diversity, Equity and Inclusion. From the human resources perspective (BasuMallick, 2020), there appeared to be five expected trends:

- Diversity will be the business model, not just a value.
- "Male Allies"—in support of WBEs—will become more popular.
- Candidates with criminal records may become more hire-able, given the EEOC win of a case where a large company used this criterion to exclude many minority candidates. This could be another chapter in itself, if we took a look at non-violent and non-financial crime statistics vs. employment rates.

- Job description language will become less "genderized" eliminating words and phrases such as aggressive, demanding, and supportive.
- Recruitment tools will become more inclusive.

In reality, D&I professionals are encountering none of the expected trends. The world has gone topsy-turvy, but: "It is in these moments where diversity and inclusion professionals challenge the status quo and make people feel comfortable being uncomfortable where real innovative change can happen." (Kaufman, 2020)

We may be at the precipice of systemic change, though it is too early to tell for sure. Wright suggests another "enlightened self-interest" light bulb moment just occurred. She believes the new DEI (Diversity, Equity and Inclusion) acronym should change to DIRE for Diversity, Inclusion, Representation, and Equity. (Wright, Vistra Director, Supply Chain Diversity, 2020) Representation at the highest levels is critical. Lack of representation sends its own negative message. If no one who looks like you is visible, it means you have no point of reference to set a goal of being in a similar position one day.

Chapter 22: At the End of the Day

Measuring Success

The simple truth is that "spend" is not an adequate measurement of the success of supplier diversity and related certification programs. Despite the fact that they are spending more with fewer diverse suppliers, most large companies are not fulfilling the mission of creating generational wealth in historically disadvantaged groups or even doing a good job of increasing market share in diverse customer communities. It's time to rethink the emphasis on spend and start bringing many more diverse companies into the mix. From a supplier diversity or supply chain perspective, the often-routine bias that a diverse company is too small to be a supplier should be flipped to ask, "Is it big enough to be a customer?" If we—your diverse business suppliers, our employees, families, and friends—are your customers, we have a vested interest in your success, and together we could be unstoppable.

Get a Piece of the Pie

To compete for that diverse spend, you have to certify. We know that diversity certification, as a process, can be overwhelmingly confusing to business owners. You have a dream, a product or service you are passionate about, that doesn't involve learning all the intricacies of certification. You want to know if you qualify, what you qualify for, and advice on the easiest way to obtain certification. You can take a simple survey at www.GetDiversityCertified.com to find out. Don't like surveys? Call or email our offices and we'll give you twenty minutes of listening and advice to point you in the right direction.

Abator's GetDiversityCertified.com consulting practice does as much, or as little, as our clients' businesses want. After intake, these custom services to legitimately diverse businesses include:

- Counselling on available certification programs based on business type and objectives
- Review of supporting documents with an emphasis on governance and control issues
- Owner(s) resume review
- Collection/verification of required documentation
- Creation and submission of complete application packages (online or paper submissions)
- Assistance in preparing responses to any certifier clarifying questions
- Pre-site visit meetings, as requested

- Notary services as appropriate

We have counselled thousands of diverse owners on certification and contracting opportunities. Our blog, aimed at the owners of small, disadvantaged/disabled, minority, women, veteran, lesbian, gay, bisexual, or transgendered business enterprises (http://blog.getdiversitycertified.com/) has been active since August of 2010, and we frequently tweet about diversity issues with the handle @DiverseBizBlog. Our team has processed applications for companies of various types, through state and federal agencies and all of the third-party certifiers. Come check us out! Together we can tackle the world.

Appendix Glossary

Certification Types

- 8(a): Federal Small Business development program
- ABE: Asian (American) Business Enterprise
- DBE: Disadvantaged Business Enterprise (**must be** socially and economically disadvantaged to qualify). ACDBEs are airport concessionaire businesses with DBE certification status.
- DWBE: Disabled Women Business Enterprise
- HUBZone: Federal designation for historically underutilized business in designated urban or rural areas or designated census tracts, the business must be located in a designated area, and 35% of its employees must live in designated HUB areas to qualify.
- LGBT: Lesbian, gay, bisexual, or transgender; sometimes appearing with a "Q" for "queer" or an "I" for "intersex" at the end; sometimes appearing with a "+" to indicate other communities beyond those indicated by the acronym (known as LGBT Business Enterprise or LGBTBE)
- MBE: Minority Business Enterprise (minorities recognized for certification in the United States are African American, Asian Pacific, Hispanic, Native

American (of all tribes including Native Hawaiian/Pacific Islander), and subcontinent Asian. Some states will break down these categories further.

- MWBE: Minority Women Business Enterprise
- PWD: Person/people with disability or disabled (known as Disability Owned Business Enterprise or DOBE)
- SBE: Small Business Enterprise
- SDMWVLGBTs: Small Disadvantaged Minority, Women, Veteran, or LQBT Businesses
- HUD Section 3: Housing and Urban Development agency-specific certification, a business must meet one of the following criteria: a) 51% of the business is owned by Section 3 residents, b) 30% of the business's current full-time staff meet the definition of a Section 3 resident, or c) business has evidence of firm commitment(s) to provide 25% of the total dollar amount of subcontracts to Section 3 businesses.
- VBE or SDVBE: Veteran or Service-Disabled Veteran Business Enterprise
- WBE: Women Business Enterprise
- WOSB/EDWOSB: Federal designation for Women-Owned Small or Economically Disadvantaged Women-Owned Small Business

Certifiers

Note: List does not include all state certifying agencies, but references the country-wide Department of Transportation (DOT)-based UCP. Information about individual state certifiers is available upon request.

- Disability:IN (formerly USBLN [US Business Leadership Network]): the 3rd party certifier for persons with disability- or disabled-owned businesses.
- EPHCC: El Paso Hispanic Chamber of Commerce, an SBA-approved certifier for the WOSB program for both WOSB and EDWOSB status.
- HUD: Housing and Urban Development, a federal agency that offers its own certification—Section 3.
- NaVOBA: National Veteran Owned Business Association, a third-party certifier of veteran- and service-disabled veteran-owned businesses.
- NGLCC: National Gay & Lesbian Chamber of Commerce, the third-party certifier for LGBT-owned businesses.
- NMSDC: National Minority Supplier Development Council, the third-party certifier for minority-owned businesses.

- NWBOC: National Women Business Owners Corporation, a third-party certifier of women-owned businesses and an SBA-approved certifier for the WOSB program for both WOSB and EDWOSB status.

- SBA: United States Small Business Administration, certifier for 8(a) and HUBZone and repository holder for the federal WOSB/EDWOSB program.

- UCP: Unified Certification Program, this program is available in every state and offers DBE certification.

- USPAACC: U.S. Pan Asian American Chamber of Commerce, third-party certifier of Asian American-owned businesses (heritage includes peoples from China, Hong Kong, Taiwan, Japan, the Philippines, South Korea, India, Indonesia, Vietnam, Cambodia, Thailand, Singapore, Malaysia, Bangladesh, Pakistan, and Mongolia).

- USWCC: U.S. Women's Chamber of Commerce, 3rd party certifier of women-owned businesses offering WBE and International WBE certification and is an SBA-approved certifier for the WOSB program for both WOSB and EDWOSB status.

- VA: formerly known as the Veterans Administration, the Department of Veterans Affairs is the federal certifier for veteran or service-disabled veteran certification. (Some states offer their own veteran-owned business certification.)

- WBENC: Women's Business Enterprise National Council, the largest 3rd party certifier of women-owned businesses and an SBA-approved certifier for the WOSB program for WOSB status only.

Other Related Acronyms

- BDR: Billion Dollar Roundtable, a group of global corporate entities working to increase commitment and spending levels with diverse suppliers.
- DUNS: Data Universal Numbering System, also known as the Dun and Bradstreet ID Number, a credit reporting number used to uniquely identify your business. A DUNS number is free from https://www.dandb.com/free-duns-number/
- FAR: Federal Acquisition Regulations, the rules governing how the federal government procures goods and services, including supplier diversity goals, which can be viewed here: https://www.acquisition.gov/?q=browsefar.
- FSC: Federal Supply Codes, a set of codes the federal government uses to "group products into logical families for management purposes."

- GSA: United States General Services Administration, they establish long-term government-wide contracts known as "GSA Schedules" (also known as "Multiple Award Schedules" or "Federal Supply Schedules"). These schedules are organized by the goods, services, or products purchased. **NOTE**: The VA has their own schedule, the VA Federal Supply Schedules Program, to procure medical supplies.

- NAICS: North American Industry Classification System, a way to classify your business (products and services sold).

- NIGP: National Institute of Governmental Purchasing Codes, a way to classify your business (products and services sold).

- OSDBU: Office of Small Disadvantaged Business Utilization, virtually every federal agency has an office to ensure use of diverse businesses similar to supplier diversity in corporate America.

- PSC: Product Service Codes, a way to classify your business (products and services sold)—these codes are broken down into three types: products, services, and research and development projects and are used in the SAM system (see below).

- SAM: System Award Management, the federal government's contracting registration system. You **MUST BE** registered to be certified by or do business with the federal government. And, to register you must have a DUNS number. SAM replaced the following disparate systems: CCR, FedReg, ORCA, and EPLS. **NOTE**: As of publication, the federal government has not completed its registration transition to Beta.SAM (https://beta.sam.gov/). Once registered in SAM, you'll be notified when the transition is complete. However, Beta.SAM has replaced the FBO (FedBizOpps) as repository for federal procurement opportunities.
- SIC: Standard Industrial Classification, a way to classify your business (products and services sold).
- TIN: Taxpayer Identification Number, also known as FEIN (Federal Employer Identification Number)
- UNSPSC: United Nations Standard Products and Services Code, a way to classify your business (products and services sold).

Appendix 2002 Redacted DOT Form

Revised 03-28-02

3

COUNTY OF ALLEGHENY, PENNSYLVANIA
MINORITY, WOMEN AND DISADVANTAGED
BUSINESS ENTERPRISE
CERTIFICATION APPLICATION

A. Company Name and Address

Name of Business: Abator Information Services, Inc.

Actual Business Address

Mailing address,
if different from business address:

2400 Ardmore Blvd., Ste. 801

City: Pittsburgh   City:

State: PA   Zip: 15221   State: Zip:

Business Telephone Number: (412) 271-5922

Business Fax Number: (412) 271-5833

B. Please circle which MBE/WBE group(s) own and control your firm

MBE

Black American
Hispanic American (If circled, circle one of the following origins)
  Mexico   Puerto Rico
  Cuban   Central America
  Portuguese
Native American (If circled, circle one of the following origins)
  American Indian   Eskimo

Aleut/Native Hawaiians (If circled, circle one of the following origins)
  Burma
  Thailand
Asian-Pacific American (If circled, circle one of the following origins)
  Japan   India
  Pakistan   Philippines
  Samoa   Guam
  Bangladesh   China
  Taiwan   Korea
  Vietnam   Laos
  Cambodia   Northern Marinas
  US Trust Territories
    of the Pacific
Burma (not a defined Minority under STAA of 1082)
Thailand (not a defined Minority under STAA of 1082)

WBE

Non-Minority
Black American
Hispanic American
  (please state origin)

Native American
  (please state origin)

Asian-Pacific
  (please state origin)

OTHER
Members of other groups
or other individuals found
to be economically
disadvantaged by the
Small Business Admin-
istration (SBA). Proof of
claim must be in the form
of statement from SBA.

Certification is **free.** *There is* **no fee** *to apply for certification as a Minority, Woman or Disadvantaged Business Enterprise with Allegheny County.*

Certify and Sell

Revised 03-28-02

C.   Company Owner Information

Name: Joanne E. Peterson

Title: President/CEO

Telephone Number: (412) 271-5922

Are you married?   Yes_____   No __X__
   i.   If so, what is your spouse's name?

   ii.   What is your spouse's affiliation to your business?

D.   Type of Ownership

( )Sole Proprietorship   ( )Joint Venture
(X)Corporation   ( )Other Entity (Explain)
( )Partnership

E.   Type of Service

Construction Contractor:
(____) General Contractor (please explain)

(____) Trades Contractor
      Plumbing _____
      Electrical _____
      Heating _____
      Flooring _____

(____) Specialty Contractor (please explain)

Certification is **free.** *There is* **no fee** *to apply for certification as a Minority, Woman or Disadvantaged Business Enterprise with Allegheny County.*

Revised 03-28-02

5

Service:
Accountant
Construction Management _____
Education _____
Health Care _____
Information Technology __X__
(Computer Services)
Insurance
Janitorial _____
Legal _____
Real Estate _____
Other (please explain) _____

(___) **Broker**
(___) **Engineer/Architect**
(___) **Manufacturer**
(___) **Supplier**

F.   Number of Years Firm Has Been in Business:

1. Please list the PRODUCTS, SERVICES and/or TYPE OF WORK your firm provides. Please be as specific as possible.
   Contingency staffing for information technology & information systems projects.

2. Please list all the equipment your firm either owns or has available for use and identify the source of the equipment. (i.e. office equipment, vehicles, tools)
   Office equipment & computer network -- source is cash payment.

3. a. How many years has your firm been in business? 19 years.

   b. How many years has your firm been in business under its present name?
   18 years.

Certification is **free.** *There is* **no fee** *to apply for certification as a Minority, Woman or Disadvantaged Business Enterprise with Allegheny County.*

Certify and Sell

Revised 03-28-02

4. List all previous names your firm has had. Avatar

5. List all previous addresses your firm has had. 303 Laurie Dr., Pgh.; PA 15235; 1601 Penn Ave.; Pgh.; PA 15221; 7207 Beacon Hill Dr., Pgh., PA 15221

6. a. Please complete the names of the owner/shareholders of the firm.

Name	Race/ Nationality	Sex	Voting %	Beneficial Ownership %	Date of Ownership	Total Cost
Female Joanne E. Peterson-Caucasian-Please see attached stock info.						
Female Wendy P. Lazzaro-Caucasian-Please see attached stock info.						
Male Charles E. Peterson-Caucasian-Please see attached stock info.						
Male Andrew S. Neilson-Caucasian-Please see attached stock info.						
Female Marian E. Neilson-Caucasian-Please see attached stock info.						

    b. How was your firm capitalized? (Submit supporting documentation)
Please see attachments.

    c. If your firm is owned in full or in part by another company, list that company and its Officers and include percentage of ownership interest. (Include complete addresses and other owned companies, if applicable.)
Not Applicable

    d. List names and addresses of any previous shareholders and percentage of shares they owned.
Not Applicable

7. If your firm has issued any shares of stock, please complete.

- The total number of authorized shares of stock for your firm
1000

- Of the authorized shares, the total number of shares that have been issued
520

- Of the issued shares, the total number of shares you own
Joanne Peterson - 350

8. List names and addresses of any previous shareholders and percentage of shares they owned.

Not Applicable

Certification is free. There is no fee to apply for certification as a Minority, Woman or Disadvantaged Business Enterprise with Allegheny County.

Revised 03-28-02

7

9. Please complete
   a. Current Board of Directors

Name	Company Position	Race/ Nationality		Date of Service
Joanne E. Peterson - CEO - Caucasian				
Wendy P. Lazzaro - Secretary - Caucasian				
Charles E. Peterson - Treasurer - Caucasian				

   b. Current Officers

Name	Company Position	Race/ Nationality	Sex	Date of Service
Same as noted in Section #9a				

10. Please list the names, addresses, and social security numbers of all Owners, Officers and Directors of the firm.

Joanne Peterson; ███████████████████
Charles Peterson; ███████████████████
Wendy Lazzaro; █████████████████████

11. List the material contributions of each owner or shareholder to the firm (i.e. equipment, real estate, cash, etc.)

Name	Description of Source	Description of Contribution	Value/ Amount	Date Acquired
Please see section # 12				

Certification is free. There is no fee to apply for certification as a Minority, Woman or Disadvantaged Business Enterprise with Allegheny County.

Certify and Sell

Revised 03-28-02

8

12. List all loans made to the firm (i.e. equipment, real estate, cash, etc.)

Person	Description of Loan	Source of Loan	Value/ Amount	Date of Loan
Charles Peterson			$13,200.00	4/89
Charles Peterson			$14,000.00	6/91
Charles Peterson			$35,000.00	2/94
Joanne Peterson			$7,000.00	1/99
Wendy Lazzaro			$5,942.00	1/98
Wendy Lazzaro			$7,000.00	1/99

13. Identify by name, race/nationality, sex and title in the firm those individuals (including owners and non-owners) who are responsible for day to day management and policy decision-making, including but not limited to those with the prime responsibility for the following:

   a. Supervision of field operations:

   Name Joanne Peterson   Title President/CEO

   Race/Nationality Caucasian   Sex F

   b. On-site project supervision:

   Name Joanne Peterson   Title President/CEO

   Race/Nationality Caucasian   Sex F

   c. Determination of what jobs the firm will undertake:

   Name Joanne Peterson   Title President/CEO

   Race/Nationality Caucasian   Sex F

   d. Hiring and firing of management personnel:

   Name Board Members   Title Please see section #F9a

   Race/Nationality   Sex

   e. Estimating:

   Name Joanne Peterson   Title President/CEO

   Race/Nationality Caucasian   Sex F

Certification is **free.** *There is* **no fee** *to apply for certification as a Minority, Woman or Disadvantaged Business Enterprise with Allegheny County.*

234

Revised 03-28-02

9

f. Marketing and sales:

Name Joanne Peterson   Title President/CEO

Race/Nationality Caucasian   Sex F

g. Purchasing of major items or supplies:

Name Wendy Lazzaro / Joanne Peterson   Title Secretary / President/CEO

Race/Nationality C aucasian (both)   Sex F (both)

h. Financial decisions:

Name Wendy Lazzaro / Joanne Peterson   Title Secretary / President/CEO

Race/Nationality Caucasian (both)   Sex F (both)

i. Negotiating and signing for:

(1) Performance/Surety Bonds

Name Not Applicable   Title

Race/Nationality   Sex

(2) Insurance

Name Wendy Lazzaro   Title Secretary

Race/Nationality Caucasian   Sex F

(3) Payroll

Name Wendy Lazzaro   Title Secretary

Race/Nationality Caucasian   Sex F

14. (a) For each of the persons listed in question 13, provide on a separate sheet of paper a description of the person's experience and number of years with the firm.
Please see attached resumes
(b) Are any of the Owners, Officers, Members of the Board of Directors or Management Officials of the firm related by blood, marriage or adoption?
Yes

15. Identify any Owners, Officers, Members of the Board of Directors or Management Officials of your firm who is or was an employee of another firm that has an ownership in your firm. What is/was their position with the other firm? Not Applicable

Certification is **free.** *There is* **no fee** *to apply for certification as a Minority, Woman or Disadvantaged Business Enterprise with Allegheny County.*

Certify and Sell

16. Indicate if this firm or other firms with any of the same Owners, Officers, Members of the Board of Directors or Management Officials have previously received or been denied certification and/or participation as a M/W/DBE and describe the circumstances. Indicate the name of the certifying authority and the date of such denial and a copy of the certification document. **Not Applicable**

BUSINESS RELATIONSHIP: For questions 17 and 18, Business Relationship is defined to include shared space, equipment, financing, employee(s), consulting, computer services, supplies.

17. Identify any Owners, Officers, Members of the Board of Directors or Management Officials of the your firm who has or had an ownership in another firm that has a business relationship with your firm. Please name the individual(s) and describe the relationship and circumstances. **Not Applicable**

18. Are any of the Owners, Officers, Members of the Board of Directors or Management Officials of your firm related by blood, marriage, or adoption to any Owners, Officers, Members of the Board of Directors or Management Officials of another with whom your firm has a present business relationship? If so, please identify the relationship. **Not Applicable**

19. List the three largest projects in dollar amounts completed by your firm during the last three years. Indicate names of prime contractors of these projects.

Project	Dollar Amount	Date Completed	Prime Contractor
Please see attached corporate references.			

List the gross income of the firm for the last three years

Year Ending:	2001	2000	1999
Gross Income:	$4,131,962	$4,316,770	$5,057,455

20. Identify your firm's current bonding company, bank and letters of credit.

Bonding Company:	Not Applicable
Bank:	Dollar Bank, NA
Letters of Credit:	Not Applicable

*Certification is **free**. There is **no fee** to apply for certification as a Minority, Woman or Disadvantaged Business Enterprise with Allegheny County.*

236

Revised 03-28-02

21. List current number of employees on payroll.

	Minority	Non-Minority	Male	Female
Full-time			3	3
Part-time			1	3

22. Are there written, oral, or tacit agreements between any persons associated in any manner with firm concerning its ownership and/or operation?

    X No
       Yes

If yes, please attach copy of written details of any such agreements.

23. Submit the following documents with the application; if unavailable, provide an explanation.

For a Corporation:
a) Current audited financial statement prepared by an independent CPA (if available). If an audited financial statement is not available, then a current financial statement for your company will be sufficient.
b) Complete, **signed** copies of prior three (3) years of **corporate** income tax returns, showing Officers' salaries and distribution of profits and/or dividends, filed with the IRS.
c) Complete, **signed** copies of prior three (3) years of **personal** income tax returns, filed with the IRS.
d) Resumes for all of the Owners and Officers of your firm.
e) Evidence (license) to do business in PA.
f) Copies of third party rental agreements (leases) and management services agreements.
g) Copy of Articles of Incorporation.
h) Copy of Corporation By-laws.
i) Record of first corporate organization meeting.
j) Copies of all stock certificates (both front and back) issued
k) Copy of stock ledger

For a Limited Liability Company (LLC):
l) Current audited financial statement prepared by an independent CPA (if available). If an audited financial statement is not available, then a current financial statement for your company will be sufficient.
m) Complete, **signed** copies of **firm's** federal income tax returns filed with the IRS, showing Officers' salaries and distribution of profits and/or dividends, for the previous three (3) years.
n) Complete, **signed** copies of **personal** federal income tax returns, filed with the IRS for the previous three (3) years.
o) Resumes for all of the Owners and Officers of your firm.
p) Evidence (license) to do business in PA.
q) Copies of third party rental agreements (leases) and management services agreements.
r) Certificate of Organization

Certification is free. *There is* no fee *to apply for certification as a Minority, Woman or Disadvantaged Business Enterprise with Allegheny County.*

237

Certify and Sell

Revised 03-28-02

s) Operating Agreement
t) Record of company's first organizational meeting.

For Partnership or Joint Venture:

a) Current audited financial statement prepared by an independent CPA (if available). If audited financial statement is not available, a current financial statement for your company will be sufficient.
b) Complete, **signed** copies of **firm's** federal income tax returns filed with the IRS, for the previous three (3) years, showing Partners' or Officers' salaries and distribution of profits and/or dividends.
c) Complete, **signed** copies of **personal** federal income tax returns filed with the IRS for the previous three (3) years.
d) Resumes for all of the Owners of your firm.
e) Evidence (license) to do business in PA.
f) Copies of third party rental agreements (leases) and management services agreements.
g) Partnership or joint venture agreement.
h) Buy-out rights.
i) Profit sharing agreement.

For Sole Proprietorship:

a) Current audited financial statement prepared by an independent CPA (if available). If an audited financial statement is not available, then a current financial statement for your company will be sufficient.
b) Complete, **signed** copies of **personal** federal income tax returns filed with the IRS, for the previous three (3) years.
c) Resume for the Owner of your firm.
d) Evidence (license) to do business in PA.
e) Copies of third party rental agreements (leases) and management services agreements.

24. If there are stipulations of:
- Stock options
- Ownership options
- Stockholder agreements
- Buy-out rights
- Stockholder voting rights
- Restrictions on the disposal of stock loan agreements
- Facts pertaining to the value of shares
- Ownership of voting securities

WHICH ARE NOT IN THE CORPORATE DOCUMENTS FURNISHED TO THE COUNTY OF ALLEGHENY, YOU ARE REQUESTED TO FURNISH COPIES OF THESE STIPULATIONS.

Certification is free. *There is* no fee *to apply for certification as a Minority, Woman or Disadvantaged Business Enterprise with Allegheny County.*

Revised 03-28-02   13

AFFIDAVIT

The undersigned does hereby swear that he or she is authorized to represent
___Abator Information Services, Inc._____(Name of firm), to
execute this affidavit on behalf of the said firm and that the foregoing statements and attachments
are true, accurate, complete and include all materials information necessary to identify and
explain the operations, control and ownership of __Abator Information Services,__
__Inc._____(Name of firm).

Further, the undersigned does covenant and agree to provide, through the prime contractor or if
there is not prime contractor, directly to the Allegheny County Office of M/W/DBE, current
complete and accurate information regarding actual work performed on the project, the payment
therefore and any proposed changes, if any, to the foregoing arrangements and to permit the audit
and examination of books, records, and files of the named firm.

Further, the undersigned acknowledges that any change in ownership, control, or financial
condition of the said firm must be brought to the attention of the Allegheny County Office of
M/W/DBE, 416 County Office Building, 542 Forbes Avenue, Pittsburgh, PA 15219 within two
weeks of the occurrence.

Further, the undersigned acknowledges that any distortion, false statements, or nondisclosure of
information will be deemed to be a material misrepresentation and is subject to prosecution under
both Federal and State law.

_____   4/18/2002
Signature   Date

SEAL.   Joanne E. Peterson
                         Printed Name

                         President/CEO
                         Title

Sworn to and subscribed
before me this _11th_ day
of _April_____, 20_02_

_____
Notary Public

My Commission Expires:

> Notarial Seal
> Janice L. McMahon, Notary Public
> Pittsburgh, Allegheny County
> My Commission Expires Feb. 10, 2003

- -

Return this application to: **Allegheny County Department of Minority, Women and
Disadvantaged Business Enterprise, 416 County Office Building, 542 Forbes Avenue,
Pittsburgh, PA 15219 Tel: (412) 350-4309 Fax: (412) 350-4915**

Certification is **free.** *There is* **no fee** *to apply for certification as a Minority,
Woman or Disadvantaged Business Enterprise with Allegheny County.*

Appendix Sample DOT Form (2019)

A. Basic Contact Information

(1) Contact person and Title: _____   (2) Legal name of firm: _____

_____   _____

(3) Phone #: ___ ____ _____   (4) Other Phone #: ___ ____ _____   (5) Fax #: ___ ____ _____

(6) E-mail: _____   (7) Firm Websites: _____

(8) Street address of firm (No P.O. Box):   City: County/Parish: State: Zip:

(9) Mailing address of firm (if different):   City: County/Parish: State: Zip:

B. Prior/Other Certifications and Applications

(10) Is your firm currently certified for any of the following U.S. DOT programs?
❑ DBE ❑ ACDBE Names of certifying agencies:

⊗ If you are certified in your home state as a DBE/ACDBE, you do not have to complete this application for other states. Ask your state UCP about the interstate certification process.

List the dates of any site visits conducted by your home state and any other states or UCP members:

Date ___ ____ ___ State/UCP Member: _____ Date ___ ____ ___ State/UCP Member: _____

(11) Indicate whether the firm or any persons listed in this application have ever been:

(a) Denied certification or decertified as a DBE, ACDBE, 8(a), SDB, MBE/WBE firm? ❑ Yes ❑ No
(b) Withdrawn an application for these programs, or debarred or suspended or otherwise had bidding privileges denied or restricted by any state or local agency, or Federal entity? ❑ Yes ❑ No

If yes, explain the nature of the action. (If you appealed the decision to DOT or another agency, attach a copy of the decision.

Section 2: GENERAL INFORMATION

A. Business Profile: (1) Give a concise description of the firm's primary activities and the product(s) or service(s) it provides. If your company offers more than one product/service, list the primary product or service first. Please use additional paper if necessary. This description may be used in our database and the UCP online directory if you are certified as a DBE or ACDBE.

(2) Applicable NAICS Codes for this line of work include: ___ ____ ____ ____ ____ ____

(3) This firm was established on ___/___/___ | (4) I/We have owned this firm since: ___/___/___

(5) Method of acquisition (Check all that apply):
❑ Started new business ❑ Bought existing business ❑ Inherited business ❑ Secured concession
❑ Merger or consolidation ❑ Other (explain)

(6) Is your firm "for profit"? ❏ Yes ❏No→   ⊗ **STOP!** If your firm is NOT for-profit, then you do NOT
Federal Tax ID# _____   qualify for this program and should not fill out this application.

(7) Type of Legal Business Structure: *(check all that apply):*
  ❏ Sole Proprietorship   ❏ Limited Liability Partnership
  ❏ Partnership   ❏Corporation
  ❏ Limited Liability Company   ❏ Joint Venture (Identify all JV partners _____)
  ❏ Applying as an ACDBE   ❏ Other, Describe

(8) Number of employees: Full-time _____ Part-time _____ Seasonal _____ Total _____
(Provide a list of employees, their job titles, and dates of employment, to your application).

(9) Specify the firm's gross receipts for the last 3 years. *(Submit complete copies of the firm's Federal tax returns for each year. If there are affiliates or subsidiaries of the applicant firm or owners, you must submit complete copies of these firms' Federal tax returns).*

Year _____ Gross Receipts of Applicant Firm $ _____ Gross Receipts of Affiliate Firms $_____
Year _____ Gross Receipts of Applicant Firm $ _____ Gross Receipts of Affiliate Firms $_____
Year _____ Gross Receipts of Applicant Firm $ _____ Gross Receipts of Affiliate Firms $_____

B. Relationships and Dealings with Other Businesses

(1) Is your firm co-located at any of its business locations, or does it share a telephone number, P.O. Box, office or storage space, yard, warehouse, facilities, equipment, inventory, financing, office staff, and/or employees with any other business, organization, or entity? ❏ Yes ❏ No
If Yes, explain the nature of your relationship with these other businesses by identifying the business or person with whom you have any formal, informal, written, or oral agreement. Also detail the items shared.

(2) Has any other firm had an ownership interest in your firm at present or at any time in the past?
❏ Yes ❏ No If Yes, explain

(3) At present, or at any time in the past, has your firm:
  (a) Ever existed under different ownership, a different type of ownership, or a different name? ❏ Yes ❏ No
  (b) Existed as a subsidiary of any other firm? ❏ Yes ❏ No
  (c) Existed as a partnership in which one or more of the partners are/were other firms? ❏ Yes ❏ No
  (d) Owned any percentage of any other firm? ❏ Yes ❏ No
  (e) Had any subsidiaries? ❏ Yes ❏ No
  (f) Served as a subcontractor with another firm constituting more than 25% of your firm's receipts? ❏ Yes ❏ No

(If you answered "Yes" to any of the questions in (2) and/or (3)(a)-(f), you may be asked to provide further details and explain whether the arrangement continues).

Certify and Sell

Section 3: MAJORITY OWNER INFORMATION

A. Identify the majority owner of the firm holding 51% or more ownership interest.

(1) Full Name:	(2) Title:	(3) Home Phone #: ( ) ___ - ___

(4) Home Address *(Street and Number)*: | City: | State: | Zip:

(5) Gender: ☐ Male ☐ Female

(6) Ethnic group membership *(Check all that apply)*:

☐ Black ☐ Hispanic
☐ Asian Pacific ☐ Native American
☐ Subcontinent Asian
☐ Other *(specify)* _____

(7) U.S. Citizenship:

☐ U.S. Citizen
☐ Lawfully Admitted Permanent Resident

(8) Number of years as owner: ___
(9) Percentage owned: _____ %
Class of stock owned: _____
Date acquired _____

(10) Initial investment to | Type | Dollar Value
acquire ownership | Cash | $
interest in firm: | Real Estate | $
| Equipment | $
| Other | $

Describe how you acquired your business:
☐ Started business myself
☐ It was a gift from: _____
☐ I bought it from: _____
☐ I inherited it from: _____
☐ Other _____

(Attach documentation substantiating your investment)

B. Additional Owner Information

(1) Describe familial relationship to other owners and employees:
_____
_____
_____

(2) Does this owner perform a management or supervisory function for any other business? ☐ Yes ☐ No
If Yes, identify: Name of Business: _____ Function/Title: _____

(3)(a) Does this owner own or work for any other firm(s) that has a relationship with this firm? *(e.g., ownership interest, shared office space, financial investments, equipment, leases, personnel sharing, etc.)* ☐ Yes ☐ No
Identify the name of the business, and the nature of the relationship, and the owner's function at the firm:
_____

(b) Does this owner work for any other firm, non-profit organization, or is engaged in any other activity more than 10 hours per week? If yes, identify this activity: _____

(4)(a) What is the personal net worth of this disadvantaged owner applying for certification ? $_____

(b)Has any trust been created for the benefit of this disadvantaged owner(s)? ☐ Yes ☐ No
(If Yes, you may be asked to provide a copy of the trust instrument).

(5) Do any of your immediate family members, managers, or employees own, manage, or are associated with another company? ☐ Yes ☐ No If Yes, provide their name, relationship, company, type of business, and indicate whether they own or manage the company: *(Please attach extra sheets, if needed):* _____

U.S. DOT Uniform DBE/ACDBE Certification Application • Page 7 of 14

Section 4: CONTROL

A. Identify your firm's Officers and Board of Directors *(If additional space is required, attach a separate sheet):*

		Name	Title	Date Appointed	Ethnicity	Gender
(1) Officers of the Company	(a)					
	(b)					
	(c)					
	(d)					
(2) Board of Directors	(a)					
	(b)					
	(c)					
	(d)					

(3) Do any of the persons listed above perform a management or supervisory function for any other business?
❏ Yes ❏ No If Yes, identify for each:

Person: _____   Title: _____
Business: _____   Function: _____

Person: _____   Title: _____
Business: _____   Function: _____

(4) Do any of the persons listed in section A above own or work for any other firm(s) that has a relationship with this firm? *(e.g., ownership interest, shared office space, financial investments, equipment, leases, personnel sharing, etc.)*
❏ Yes ❏ No If Yes, identify for each:

Firm Name: _____   Person: _____
Nature of Business Relationship: _____

B. Duties of Owners, Officers, Directors, Managers, and Key Personnel
1. *(Identify your firm's management personnel who control your firm in the following areas (Attach separate sheets as needed).*

A= Always S = Seldom F = Frequently N = Never	Majority Owner (51% or more) Name: _____ Title: _____ Percent Owned:				Minority Owner (49% or less) Name: _____ Title: _____ Percent Owned:			
Sets policy for company direction/scope of operations	A ❏	F ❏	S ❏	N ❏	A ❏	F ❏	S ❏	N ❏
Bidding and estimating	A ❏	F ❏	S ❏	N ❏	A ❏	F ❏	S ❏	N ❏
Major purchasing decisions	A ❏	F ❏	S ❏	N ❏	A ❏	F ❏	S ❏	N ❏
Marketing and sales	A ❏	F ❏	S ❏	N ❏	A ❏	F ❏	S ❏	N ❏
Supervises field operations	A ❏	F ❏	S ❏	N ❏	A ❏	F ❏	S ❏	N ❏
Attend bid opening and lettings	A ❏	F ❏	S ❏	N ❏	A ❏	F ❏	S ❏	N ❏
Perform office management (billing, accounts receivable/payable, etc.)	A ❏	F ❏	S ❏	N ❏	A ❏	F ❏	S ❏	N ❏
Hires and fires management staff	A ❏	F ❏	S ❏	N ❏	A ❏	F ❏	S ❏	N ❏
Hire and fire field staff or crew	A ❏	F ❏	S ❏	N ❏	A ❏	F ❏	S ❏	N ❏
Designates profits spending or investment	A ❏	F ❏	S ❏	N ❏	A ❏	F ❏	S ❏	N ❏
Obligates business by contract/credit	A ❏	F ❏	S ❏	N ❏	A ❏	F ❏	S ❏	N ❏
Purchase equipment	A ❏	F ❏	S ❏	N ❏	A ❏	F ❏	S ❏	N ❏
Signs business checks	A ❏	F ❏	S ❏	N ❏	A ❏	F ❏	S ❏	N ❏

U.S. DOT Uniform DBE/ACDBE Certification Application • Page 9 of 14

243

2. Complete for all Officers, Directors, Managers, and Key Personnel who control the following functions for the firm. *(Attach separate sheets as needed).*

A = Always S = Seldom F = Frequently N = Never	Officer/Director/Manager/Key Personnel Name: _____ Title: _____ Race and Gender: _____ Percent Owned:				Officer/Director/Manager/ Key Personnel Name: _____ Title: _____ Race and Gender: _____ Percent Owned:			
Sets policy for company direction/scope of operations	A ☐	F ☐	S ☐	N ☐	A ☐	F ☐	S ☐	N ☐
Bidding and estimating	A ☐	F ☐	S ☐	N ☐	A ☐	F ☐	S ☐	N ☐
Major purchasing decisions	A ☐	F ☐	S ☐	N ☐	A ☐	F ☐	S ☐	N ☐
Marketing and sales	A ☐	F ☐	S ☐	N ☐	A ☐	F ☐	S ☐	N ☐
Supervises field operations	A ☐	F ☐	S ☐	N ☐	A ☐	F ☐	S ☐	N ☐
Attend bid opening and lettings	A ☐	F ☐	S ☐	N ☐	A ☐	F ☐	S ☐	N ☐
Perform office management (billing, accounts receivable/payable, etc.)	A ☐	F ☐	S ☐	N ☐	A ☐	F ☐	S ☐	N ☐
Hires and fires management staff	A ☐	F ☐	S ☐	N ☐	A ☐	F ☐	S ☐	N ☐
Hire and fire field staff or crew	A ☐	F ☐	S ☐	N ☐	A ☐	F ☐	S ☐	N ☐
Designates profits spending or investment	A ☐	F ☐	S ☐	N ☐	A ☐	F ☐	S ☐	N ☐
Obligates business by contract/credit	A ☐	F ☐	S ☐	N ☐	A ☐	F ☐	S ☐	N ☐
Purchase equipment	A ☐	F ☐	S ☐	N ☐	A ☐	F ☐	S ☐	N ☐
Signs business checks	A ☐	F ☐	S ☐	N ☐	A ☐	F ☐	S ☐	N ☐

Do any of the persons listed in B1 or B2 perform a management or supervisory function for any other business? If Yes, identify the person, the business, and their title/function: _____
_____

Do any of the persons listed above own or work for any other firm(s) that has a relationship with this firm? *(e.g. ownership interest, shared office space, financial investments, equipment, leases, personnel sharing, etc.)* If Yes, describe the nature of the business relationship:_____
_____

C. Inventory: Indicate your firm's inventory in the following categories *(Please attach additional sheets if needed)*:

1. Equipment and Vehicles

Make and Model	Current Value	Owned or Leased by Firm or Owner?	Used as collateral?	Where is item stored?

1. _____
2. _____
3. _____
4. _____
5. _____
6. _____
7. _____
8. _____
9. _____

2. Office Space

Street Address	Owned or Leased by Firm or Owner?	Current Value of Property or Lease

_____
_____
_____

3. Storage Space *(Provide signed lease agreements for the properties listed)*

Street Address	Owned or Leased by Firm or Owner?	Current Value of Property or Lease

D. Does your firm rely on any other firm for management functions or employee payroll? ❑ Yes ❑ No

E. Financial/Banking Information *(Provide bank authorization and signature cards)*

Name of bank: _____ City and State: _____
The following individuals are able to sign checks on this account: _____

Name of bank: _____ City and State: _____
The following individuals are able to sign checks on this account: _____

Bonding Information: If you have bonding capacity, identify the firm's bonding aggregate and project limits:
Aggregate limit $ _____ Project limit $ _____

F. Identify all sources, amounts, and purposes of money loaned to your firm including from financial institutions. Identify whether you the owner and any other person or firm loaned money to the applicant DBE/ACDBE. Include the names of any persons or firms guaranteeing the loan, if other than the listed owner.
(Provide copies of signed loan agreements and security agreements).

Name of Source	Address of Source	Name of Person Guaranteeing the Loan	Original Amount	Current Balance	Purpose of Loan
1.					
2.					
3.					

G. List all contributions or transfers of assets to/from your firm and to/from any of its owners or another individual over the past two years *(Attach additional sheets if needed)*:

Contribution/Asset	Dollar Value	From Whom Transferred	To Whom Transferred	Relationship	Date of Transfer
1.					
2.					
3.					

H. List current licenses/permits held by any owner and/or employee of your firm
(e.g. contractor, engineer, architect, etc.)(Attach additional sheets if needed):

Name of License/Permit Holder	Type of License/Permit	Expiration Date	State
1.			
2.			
3.			

U.S. DOT Uniform DBE/ACDBE Certification Application • Page 11 of 14

Certify and Sell

I. List the three largest contracts completed by your firm in the past three years, if any:

Name of Owner/Contractor	Name/Location of Project	Type of Work Performed	Dollar Value of Contract
1.			
2.			
3.			

J. List the three largest active jobs on which your firm is currently working:

Name of Prime Contractor and Project Number	Location of Project	Type of Work	Project Start Date	Anticipated Completion Date	Dollar Value of Contract
1.					
2.					
3.					

AIRPORT CONCESSION (ACDBE) APPLICANTS ONLY MUST COMPLETE THIS SECTION

Identify the following information concerning the ACDBE applicant firm:

Concession Space	Address / Location at Airport	Value of Property or Lease	Fees/Lease Payments Paid to the Airport

Provide information concerning any other airport concession businesses the applicant firm or any affiliate owns and/or operates, including name, location, type of concession, and start date of concession

Name of Concession	Location	Type of Concession	Start Date of Concession

U.S. DOT Uniform DBE/ACDBE Certification Application • Page 12 of 14

246

AFFIDAVIT OF CERTIFICATION

This form must be signed and notarized for each owner upon which disadvantaged status is relied.

A MATERIAL OR FALSE STATEMENT OR OMISSION MADE IN CONNECTION WITH THIS APPLICATION IS SUFFICIENT CAUSE FOR DENIAL OF CERTIFICATION, REVOCATION OF A PRIOR APPROVAL, INITIATION OF SUSPENSION OR DEBARMENT PROCEEDINGS, AND MAY SUBJECT THE PERSON AND/OR ENTITY MAKING THE FALSE STATEMENT TO ANY AND ALL CIVIL AND CRIMINAL PENALTIES AVAILABLE PURSUANT TO APPLICABLE FEDERAL AND STATE LAW.

I _____ (full name printed), swear or affirm under penalty of law that I am _____ (title) of the applicant firm _____ and that I have read and understood all of the questions in this application and that all of the foregoing information and statements submitted in this application and its attachments and supporting documents are true and correct to the best of my knowledge, and that all responses to the questions are full and complete, omitting no material information. The responses include all material information necessary to fully and accurately identify and explain the operations, capabilities and pertinent history of the named firm as well as the ownership, control, and affiliations thereof.

I recognize that the information submitted in this application is for the purpose of inducing certification approval by a government agency. I understand that a government agency may, by means it deems appropriate, determine the accuracy and truth of the statements in the application, and I authorize such agency to contact any entity named in the application, and the named firm's bonding companies, banking institutions, credit agencies, contractors, clients, and other certifying agencies for the purpose of verifying the information supplied and determining the named firm's eligibility.

I agree to submit to government audit, examination and review of books, records, documents and files, in whatever form they exist, of the named firm and its affiliates, inspection of its places(s) of business and equipment, and to permit interviews of its principals, agents, and employees. I understand that refusal to permit such inquiries shall be grounds for denial of certification.

If awarded a contract, subcontract, concession lease or sublease, I agree to promptly and directly provide the prime contractor, if any, and the Department, recipient agency, or federal funding agency on an ongoing basis, current, complete and accurate information regarding (1) work performed on the project; (2) payments; and (3) proposed changes, if any, to the foregoing arrangements.

I agree to provide written notice to the recipient agency or Unified Certification Program of any material change in the information contained in the original application within 30 calendar days of such change (e.g., ownership changes, address/telephone number, personal net worth exceeding $1.32 million, etc.).

I acknowledge and agree that any misrepresentations in this application or in records pertaining to a contract or subcontract will be grounds for terminating any contract or subcontract which may be awarded; denial or revocation of certification; suspension and debarment; and for initiating action under federal and/or state law concerning false statement, fraud or other applicable offenses.

I certify that I am a socially and economically disadvantaged individual who is an owner of the above-referenced firm seeking certification as a Disadvantaged Business Enterprise or Airport Concession Disadvantaged Business Enterprise. In support of my application, I certify that I am a member of one or more of the following groups, and that I have held myself out as a member of the group(s): (Check all that apply):

❏ Female ❏ Black American ❏ Hispanic American
❏ Native American ❏ Asian-Pacific American
❏ Subcontinent Asian American ❏ Other (specify)

_____

I certify that I am socially disadvantaged because I have been subjected to racial or ethnic prejudice or cultural bias, or have suffered the effects of discrimination, because of my identity as a member of one or more of the groups identified above, without regard to my individual qualities.

I further certify that my personal net worth does not exceed $1.32 million, and that I am economically disadvantaged because my ability to compete in the free enterprise system has been impaired due to diminished capital and credit opportunities as compared to others in the same or similar line of business who are not socially and economically disadvantaged.

I declare under penalty of perjury that the information provided in this application and supporting documents is true and correct.

Signature _____ _____
      (DBE/ACDBE Applicant)   (Date)

NOTARY CERTIFICATE

U.S. DOT Uniform DBE/ACDBE Certification Application • Page 13 of 14

U.S. Department of Transportation	**Personal Net Worth Statement** **For DBE/ACDBE Program Eligibility** As of _____	OMB APPROVAL NO: EXPIRATION DATE:

This form is used by all participants in the U.S. Department of Transportation's Disadvantaged Business Enterprise (DBE) Programs. Each individual owner of a firm applying to participate as a DBE or ACDBE, whose ownership and control are relied upon for DBE certification must complete this form. Each person signing this form authorizes the Unified Certification Program (UCP) recipient to make inquiries as necessary to verify the accuracy of the statements made. The agency you apply to will use the information provided to determine whether an owner is economically disadvantaged as defined in the DBE program regulations 49 C.F.R. Parts 23 and 26. **Return form to appropriate UCP certifying member, not U.S. DOT.**

Name		Business Phone
Residence Address (As reported to the IRS) City, State and Zip Code		Residence Phone
Business Name of Applicant Firm		
Spouse's Full Name (Marital Status: Single, Married, Divorced, Union)		

ASSETS	(Omit Cents)	LIABILITIES	(Omit Cents)
Cash and Cash Equivalents	$	Loan on Life Insurance (Complete Section 5)	$
Retirement Accounts (IRAs, 401Ks, 403Bs, Pensions, etc.) (Report full value minus tax and interest penalties that would apply if assets were distributed today) (Complete Section 3)	$	Mortgages on Real Estate Excluding Primary Residence Debt (Complete Section 4)	$
Brokerage, Investment Accounts	$	Notes, Obligations on Personal Property (Complete Section 6)	$
Assets Held in Trust	$	Notes & Accounts Payable to Banks and Others (Complete Section 2)	$
Loans to Shareholders & Other Receivables (Complete section 6)	$	Other Liabilities (Complete Section 8)	$
Real Estate Excluding Primary Residence (Complete Section 4)	$	Unpaid Taxes (Complete Section 8)	$
Life Insurance (Cash Surrender Value Only) (Complete Section 5)	$		
Other Personal Property and Assets (Complete Section 6)	$		
Business Interests Other Than the Applicant Firm (Complete Section 7)	$		
Total Assets	$	Total Liabilities	$
		NET WORTH	

Section 2. Notes Payable to Banks and Others

Name of Noteholder(s)	Original Balance	Current Balance	Payment Amount	Frequency (monthly, etc.)	How Secured or Endorsed Type of Collateral

U.S. DOT Personal Net Worth Statement for DBE/ACDBE Program Eligibility • Page 1 of 5

Section 3. Brokerage and custodial accounts, stocks, bonds, retirement accounts. (Full Value) (Use attachments if necessary).

Name of Security / Brokerage Account / Retirement Account	Cost	Market Value Quotation/Exchange	Date of Quotation/Exchange	Total Value

Section 4. Real Estate Owned (Including Primary Residence, Investment Properties, Personal Property Leased or Rented for Business Purposes, Farm Properties, or any Other Income Producing property). (List each parcel separately. Add additional sheets if necessary).

	Primary Residence	Property B	Property C
Type of Property			
Address			
Date Acquired and Method of Acquisition (purchase, inherit, divorce, gift, etc.)			
Names on Deed			
Purchase Price			
Present Market Value			
Source of Market Valuation			
Name of all Mortgage Holders			
Mortgage Acc. # and balance (as of date of form)			
Equity line of credit balance			
Amount of Payment Per Month/Year (Specify)			

Section 5. Life Insurance Held (Give face amount and cash surrender value of policies, name of insurance company and beneficiaries).

Insurance Company	Face Value	Cash Surrender Amount	Beneficiaries	Loan on Policy Information

Certify and Sell

Section 6. Other Personal Property and Assets (Use attachments as necessary)

Type of Property or Asset	Total Present Value	Amount of Liability (Balance)	Is this asset insured?	Lien or Note amount and Terms of Payment
Automobiles and Vehicles (including recreation vehicles, motorcycles, boats, etc.) Include personally owned vehicles that are leased or rented to businesses or other individuals.				
Household Goods / Jewelry				
Other (List)				
Accounts and Notes Receivables				

Section 7. Value of Other Business Investments, Other Businesses Owned (excluding applicant firm)
Sole Proprietorships, General Partners, Joint Ventures, Limited Liability Companies, Closely-held and Public Traded Corporations

Section 8. Other Liabilities and Unpaid Taxes (Describe)

Section 9. Transfer of Assets: Have you within 2 years of this personal net worth statement, transferred assets to a spouse, domestic partner, relative, or entity in which you have an ownership or beneficial interest including a trust? Yes ☐ No ☐ If yes, describe.

I declare under penalty of perjury that the information provided in this personal net worth statement and supporting documents is complete, true and correct. I certify that no assets have been transferred to any beneficiary for less than fair market value in the last two years. I recognize that the information submitted in this application is for the purpose of inducing certification approval by a government agency. I understand that a government agency may, by means it deems appropriate, determine the accuracy and truth of the statements in the application and this personal net worth statement, and I authorize such agency to contact any entity named in the application or this personal financial statement, including the names banking institutions, credit agencies, contractors, clients, and other certifying agencies for the purpose of verifying the information supplied and determining the named firm's eligibility. I acknowledge and agree that any misrepresentations in this application or in records pertaining to a contract or subcontract will be grounds for terminating any contract or subcontract which may be awarded; denial or revocation of certification; suspension and debarment; and for initiating action under federal and/or state law concerning false statement, fraud or other applicable offenses.

NOTARY CERTIFICATE:
(Insert applicable state acknowledgment, affirmation, or oath)

_____   _____
Signature (DBE/ACDBE Owner)   Date

In collecting the information requested by this form, the Department of Transportation complies with Federal Freedom of Information and Privacy Act (5 U.S.C. 552 and 552a) provisions. The Privacy Act provides comprehensive protections for your personal information. This includes how information is collected, used, disclosed, stored, and discarded. Your information will not be disclosed to third parties without your consent. The information collected will be used solely to determine your firm's eligibility to participate in the Disadvantaged Business Enterprise (DBE) Program or Airport Concessionaire DBE Programs as defined in 49 C.F.R. Parts 23 and 26. You may review DOT's complete Privacy Act Statement in the Federal Register published on April 11, 2000 (65 FR 19477).

U.S. DOT Personal Net Worth Statement for DBE/ACDBE Program Eligibility • Page 3 of 5

Appendix DOT Unified Certification Supporting Documents

All Businesses

- Work experience resumes (that include places of ownership/employment with corresponding dates) for all owners, officers, and key personnel of your firm

- Personal financial statement (form available with this application) for each socially and economically disadvantaged owner comprising the 51% or more of the ownership percentage of the firm.

- Past three years federal personal tax returns (all related schedules for the past three years), for each owner claiming disadvantaged status

- Firm's federal tax returns (gross receipts) and all related schedules (including requests for extensions) for the past three years, and those filed by its affiliates

- Documented proof of contributions used to acquire ownership for each owner (e.g. both sides of cancelled checks)

- Signed loan agreements, security agreements, and bonding forms

- List of company-owned equipment and vehicles owned or leased, including VINs, copies of titles, proof of ownership, and insurance cards for each vehicle
- Title(s), registration certificate(s), and U.S. DOT numbers for each truck owned or operated by your firm
- Licenses, license renewal forms, permits, and haul authority forms
- Descriptions of all real estate (including office/storage space, etc.) owned/leased by your firm and documented proof of ownership/signed leases
- Documented proof of any transfers of assets to/from your firm and/or to/from any of its owners over the past two years
- DBE/ACDBE and SBA 8(a), SDB, MBE/WBE certifications, denials, and/or de-certifications, if applicable
- Bank authorization and signatory cards
- Schedule of salaries (or other compensation or remuneration) paid to all officers, managers, owners, and/or directors of the firm
- List of all employees, job titles, and dates of employment
- Proof of warehouse/storage facility ownership or lease arrangement

Partnership or Joint Venture

- Original and any amended partnership or joint venture agreements

Corporation or LLC

- Official Articles of Incorporation (signed by the state official)
- Both sides of all corporate stock certificates and your firm's stock transfer ledger
- Shareholders' agreement
- Minutes of **ALL** stockholders and board of directors meetings
- Corporate bylaws and any amendments
- Corporate bank resolution and bank signature cards
- Official Certificate of Formation and Operating Agreement with any amendments (for LLCs)

Suppliers

List of product lines carried and list of distribution equipment owned and/or leased

May Be Requested

We recommend providing when applying:

- Proof of citizenship or legal residency status
- Insurance agreements for each truck owned or operated by your firm
- Personal federal tax returns for the past three years, if applicable, for other disadvantaged owners of the firm
- Audited financial statements (if available)
- Trust agreements held by any owner claiming disadvantaged status, if any
- Year-end balance sheets and income statements for the past three years (or life of firm, if less than three years); a new business **must** provide a current balance sheet

Appendix Disadvantage Narrative

One of the most difficult tasks that can be undertaken is the narrative of social and economic disadvantage that may be required for SBA 8(a) or DBE certification. In this narrative, you must write about your personal experiences and how these experiences have had a negative impact on your ability to achieve expected outcomes. This can include educational, financial, racial, gender, geographical, and employment-related events throughout your life. This guide is intended to help you prepare your own narrative.

1. Select the issues you perceive are the reasons you have experienced professional rejection:

   _____ Ethnic origin   _____ Gender

   _____ Disability   _____ Race

   _____ Residence   _____ Education

   _____ Other, describe:

2. Do you believe you were ever denied admission to a college, university or other educational institution for

different criteria than those criteria which were required of other individuals of equivalent qualification and that this denial has had a negative impact of your ability to enter or advance in business?

3. Do you believe you were ever excluded from joining any educational clubs, fraternities, or professional organizations and that this exclusion has had a negative impact on your ability to enter or advance in business?

4. Do you believe the school, college, or university that you attended seriously lacked qualified teachers, staff, facilities, or equipment to the extent that it had a negative effect on the quality of your education?

5. Were you ever denied educational honors or recognition for reasons that were different than those provided to other individuals of equivalent qualification and that this denial has had a negative impact on your ability to enter or advance in business?

6. Were you ever denied a scholarship or other financial support required to finance your education for reasons that were different than those provided to other individuals of equivalent qualification and that this denial has had a negative impact on your ability to enter or advance in business?

7. Were you ever directed or led into a specific "learning track" for reasons that were different than those provided to other individuals of equivalent qualification, and did this direction have a negative impact on your ability to enter or advance in business?

8. Were you ever denied admission to any school, college, or university because of your long-term residence in a community isolated from the mainstream of American society?

9. Were you ever denied professional training in your work that has impaired your entry or advancement in your professional career?

10. Were you ever subjected to harassment in your educational environment that negatively affected your learning and entry or advancement in the business world?

11. Were you ever subjected to social pressures that discouraged you from pursuing professional or higher education or to select career opportunities that might naturally prepare you for business ownership? Did these pressures have a negative impact on your ability to enter or advance in business?

12. Were you ever denied access to mentoring, on-the-job training, apprenticeships, etc. required to gain the

necessary skills to advance in your field that has had a negative impact on your ability to enter or advance in business?

13. Were you ever subjected to significant variations in salary and/or fringe benefits from those of equally qualified contemporaries that had a negative impact on your ability to enter or advance in business?

14. Were you ever denied salary increases, bonuses, or commissions for reasons that were different than those required of other individuals of equivalent qualification, and did this denial have a negative impact on your ability to enter or advance in business?

15. Have you ever experienced low-income status for reasons that were different than those required of other individuals of equivalent qualification, and has this experience had a negative impact on your ability to enter or advance in business?

16. Were you ever terminated for reasons that were different than those applied to other individuals of equivalent qualifications? And, has this termination(s) had a negative impact on your ability to enter or advance in business?

17. Have you ever experienced harassment in your work environment such that it had a negative impact on your

job performance and your entry or advancement in the business world?

18. Have you experienced a "glass ceiling" for reasons that were different than those applied to other individuals of equivalent qualifications that kept you from advancement into management positions?

19. Have you ever been excluded from participating in company groups or functions for reasons different than those applied to other similarly situated individuals which had a negative impact on your ability to enter or advance in business?

20. Have you ever been denied employment opportunities for reasons different than those applied to others who were not socially disadvantaged individuals?

21. Have you ever been denied access to contract bidding opportunities for reasons that were different than those required of other equivalently qualified individuals, which has had a negative impact on your ability to enter or advance in business?

22. Have you ever been unfairly denied the award of a contract for reasons that were different than those required of other equivalently qualified individuals and which negatively affected your entry or advancement in the business world?

23. Have you ever been kept from joining in teaming or subcontracting relationships for reasons that were different than those required of other equivalently qualified individuals and which negatively affected your entry or advancement in the business world?

24. Have you ever been subjected to negotiations regarding issues that were different than those required of other equivalently qualified individuals and which negatively affected your entry or advancement in the business world?

25. Have you ever been systematically excluded from access to facilities where business is normally conducted for reasons that were different than those required of other equivalently qualified individuals, which negatively affected your entry or advancement in the business world?

26. Have you ever been unfairly excluded from participation in professional or business groups for reasons that were different than those required of other equivalently qualified individuals and which negatively affected your entry or advancement in the business world?

27. Have you or your company been negatively characterized for unsatisfactory past performance for

reasons that were different than those required of other equivalently qualified individuals and which negatively affected your entry or advancement in the business world?

28. Have you been denied access to private-sector or government decision makers, contacting officers or buyers for reasons that were different than those required of other equivalently qualified individuals and which negatively affected your entry or advancement in the business world?

29. Have you ever been denied access to the capital or credit necessary to operate and grow your business for reasons that were different than those required of other equivalently qualified individuals and which negatively affected your entry or advancement in the business world?

30. Have you ever been denied bonding, licenses, or leases necessary to operate and grow your business for reasons that were different than those required of other equivalently qualified individuals and which negatively affected your entry or advancement in the business world?

31. Have you or your company ever been denied a performance or any other type of bond needed to

acquire or perform work based on criteria that were less favorable in amount and terms than required of other similar companies who are not socially and economically disadvantaged?

32. Was the level of bonding that you received less favorable in amount and terms than that of other similar companies who are not socially and economically disadvantaged?

33. Have you or your company ever been denied the required credit or financing needed to acquire necessary equipment, etc. or to finance the ongoing operations of your company based on criteria terms; e.g., interest rate, collateral, etc., that were less favorable in amount and terms than required of other similar companies who are not socially and economically disadvantaged?

34. Have you or your company ever been denied a license required by you to conduct business based on criteria that were less favorable than required of other similar companies who are not socially and economically disadvantaged?

35. Have you or your company ever had a necessary license revoked based on criteria that were less favorable than

required of other similar companies who are not socially and economically disadvantaged?

36. Has your company ever been denied a real or tangible property lease based on criteria that were less favorable than required of other similar companies who are not socially and economically disadvantaged?

37. Were the terms of your leases less favorable than those received by similar companies who are not socially and economically disadvantaged?

38. Have you or your company ever been denied access to a client or to bidding on a contract opportunity based on criteria that were less favorable than required of other similar companies who are not socially and economically disadvantaged?

39. Has your firm ever been rejected for a business opportunity on terms that were different than those provided to other similar firms that were not socially and economically disadvantaged?

40. Have you ever been denied employment or advancement opportunities for reasons that were less favorable than required of equivalently qualified individuals that negatively impacted your economic situation?

41. Have you ever been discharged, fired, or down-sized on terms that were different than those provided to other equivalently qualified individuals?

We recommend that, for each question you answered with "yes," you complete a statement in your own words detailing your experiences. You should be as specific as possible, mentioning examples, and provide supporting documentation:

I have personally experienced specific, chronic, and significant instances of social disadvantage because I was subjected to social pressures that discouraged me from pursuing professional or higher education or career opportunities that would help prepare me for business ownership. CITE SPECIFIC EXAMPLES. This has negatively affected my entry or advancement into the business world.

If there is a ruling by a court or administrative board that determined you were the victim of discrimination in these experiences, you should attach a copy of each judgment or order to your narrative (or SBA Form).

Sometimes you don't have documentation—Joanne certainly didn't—but she did have a history based on her era and a disability. So, here are some excerpts from our 2004 8(a) application:

Economic disadvantage:

Access to capital is limited on both personal and professional level. Despite having my own job, my then husband was asked to co-sign automobile loans (Winters Bank, Dayton Ohio) and credit could not be held in my name alone. Upon starting a business, credit was unavailable without husband's co-signature despite his lack of involvement in the business (Mellon Bank). Due to his fear of my failure, he insisted on a post-nuptial agreement to limit risk on "his" property. As a divorced woman it took years to build credit-worthiness in the eyes of lending institutions in western Pennsylvania."

Social disadvantage:

All along, it seems I have chosen the non-traditional path, becoming a member of elite groups as women represent less than 25% of all computer programmers or software engineers and only 21.7% of chief executives. While it is clear that under the law women are equal in economic rights, the reality is different. Due to biological, physical, health, educational status, etc., it appears that fewer women than men have access to opportunities. Physically speaking, those who are partially handicapped face sometimes overwhelming odds in establishing and running small businesses. We're taken less seriously than those who appear whole. Educationally speaking, I was not encouraged to seek higher education beyond clerical/retail training – "suitable female occupations" by my parents, and my first semester at Grahm Jr. College, September 1971, was in retail.

In 1975-6, I filed an EEOC complaint against Cutler Williams of Dallas, Texas; a now defunct supplier of services similar to Abator's. I had discovered that my new boss hired his brother, paid him about $5000 per year more and required that I train the fellow to do my job. Three months into the training, this gentleman terminated me saying "you don't fit the image Cutler Williams wants to portray." I believe he was referring to the fact that I was short and overweight – of course, he could have meant I was female, and in fact, I was the only female in the recruiting department. This EEOC complaint was subsequently withdrawn because I had taken a job in Ohio (Allen Services, Inc.), and could not afford the costs of following through and was counter-sued by Cutler Williams for taking a position which they believed to be in conflict with onerous non-compete agreements. Cutler Williams sued several individuals who had taken positions with Allen Services Corporation (a now defunct supplier of similar services); suits which were subsequently dismissed for a variety of reasons.

During the first eight years of my career I repeatedly discovered that both I and my very few women co-workers were consistently paid less than males in the same or similar positions, while women were generally required to work more hours. (Cutler Williams - Dallas, Automation Consultants Inc. and Allen Services both of Dayton, OH). Management's first choice was the promotion of men, because they cited "customers preferred to deal with male counterparts" both at the technical and administrative support levels ...

I was terminated from one position because the boss stated that my "impending marriage" meant I was no longer "... committed to long term employment or career advancement" (Automation Consultants, Inc., Spring 1978). Maternity leave was virtually unheard of in that era, and I was required to be on the phone within 3 hours of giving birth to answer a manager's questions about issues left on my desk (Allen Services, MA750A and H-1 visa applications for Chrysler Project, 1979).

Despite my mother's vocal opposition, I enrolled part-time at Chatham College in 1980. It was her belief that my further education was unnecessary despite the fact that a Westinghouse contract manager advised me that no one at

Westinghouse would be allowed to hire me without a four degree. I managed to obtain a BA, finishing the equivalent of 2 years education over a six-year period.

In 1983, Consultant Systems, Inc. of Toledo, OH for whom I established and ran the eastern divisional office (1980 to early April 1983) "closed" its Pittsburgh office. They laid off the two female employees but retained the only male.

When founding Abator in 1983, funding was difficult to find based upon the then extremely limited access to capital for women. In fact, there was no capital available that Spring, so the only alternative became to be an independent sales agent for yet another competitor, – Azatar Computer Systems of Rochester, NY. Ronald Regan espoused a program in 1984 – 12 months after starting the company – that was geared to encouraging lending institutions to finance WBEs. Unfortunately, lots of hype was given to the program but I personally saw no difference at the time, and funded Abator from my Azatar commissions. I obtained a small personal credit line through Mellon Bank Monroeville Branch in 1984 which later became a $10,000 corporate line when I transferred the assets of the sole-proprietorship to the newly incorporated Abator. This was further exacerbated in 1985-86, when Abator's accounts receivable-based line of credit *was unable to grow with its business growth. It took two years to find a bank with a small business group that made its loans based on merit and repayment history rather than the lack of a gender-based track record; by which time I had maxed out my credit cards to keep the business running.*

Appendix FTC Complaint

31 July 2007

Reference # 1178888

Ms. Deborah Platt Majoras, Chairman

Federal Trade Commission
600 Pennsylvania Avenue, N.W.
Washington, D.C. 20580

Dear Ms. Majoras:

After completing its due diligence tasks, Abator Information Services (Abator) entered into an agreement with Albet Enterprises, Inc. (Albet) of 2675 E. Flamingo Road, Suite 6; Las Vegas, Nevada 89121 in early March 2007. This agreement was based upon Albet's August 2006 solicitation of Abator. Albet was to connect and provide marketing services to assist their Tribal 8(a) Teaming Partner – believed to be Home Media Technologies (HMT) - and Abator as primary teaming partner in obtaining federal contracts under specific NAICS codes. Abator primary codes include: 541511, 541512, 541519, 514210, 561300.

To date, the majority of pre-paid items promised by Albet have not been received. Abator acknowledges that it has not made its third and final payment, on the basis of mitigating circumstances.

Abator invited Albet (and therefore, HMT) to participate in a U.S. Navy opportunity as a subcontractor based on Abator's GSA ITS70 contract vehicle and Abator's own 8(a) Women Business Enterprise status. Abator has been awarded a purchase order as a result of its proposal.

During the process of preparing its proposal, Abator learned of what it believes is misleading, if not fraudulent, activities in the Albet/Tribal 8(a) partnering program. We have now had communication with other small businesses that appear to have similar concerns. Abator's attorney suggested that we notify the FTC of these concerns.

Abator is not registering this complaint over the $5184.00 paid to Albet for undelivered services. We believe there are hundreds of small businesses in various disciplines (NAICS codes) located throughout the U.S. targeted last summer via the federal Central Contractor Registry. Each of these businesses will have been told that they were *"being granted the opportunity to be the **Primary Teaming Partner** via ALBET"* if certain conditions are met. Specifically, a quick turnaround of payment to Albet and then the company is asked to spend money for NAICS code searches through a vendor recommended by Albet and asked to share its customer contact information with Albet.

Abator has a complete record of all communications with Albet, and with at least two other companies, should the FTC have any interest in acquiring copies of these records.

Sincerely,

Joanne E. Peterson
President/CEO

Abator ... IT Services since 1984
800-544-1210 or collect 412-271-5922
Fax: 412-271-5833
www.abator.com
www.lolopop.net

CCR/Pronet Cage: 1UQC9
GSA FSS ITS70 GS-35F-0388P

Certify and Sell

Certified SDB/WBE/DBE

SBA 8(a) 110912
WBENC National WBE Certification 0534
Multiple state and county certifications available upon request.

Joanne Peterson & Marian Neilson

21 August 2007

Reference # 1178888

Ms. Linda Henry, Investigator
Federal Trade Commission
Mail drop H286
Washington, DC 20580

Dear Ms. Henry,

Please note that your letter of 18 August 2007 includes a mischaracterization. Abator was awarded its contract with the U.S. Navy as a result of Abator's twenty-four years of excellent past performance in commercial and government contracting.

Our complaint has nothing to do with the USN acquisition and award, but the discoveries made regarding Albet business practices that were derived as a result of inviting Albet to participate in Abator's process.

Abator's concern is that Albet used the CCR to contact small businesses with a proposition that is essentially dishonest; violating truth in advertising standards and, perhaps, participating in fraudulent multilevel marketing. Our complaint involves multiple participants and we would be happy to share contact information with you should the FTC determine it is in the best interests of U.S. small businesses to investigate the matter further.

Best Regards,

Joanne E. Peterson
President/CEO

Abator ... IT Services since 1984
800-544-1210 or collect 412-271-5922
Fax: 412-271-5833
www.abator.com
www.lolopop.net

CCR/Pronet Cage: 1UQC9
GSA FSS ITS70 GS-35F-0388P

Certify and Sell

Certified SDB/WBE/DBE
SBA 8(a) 110912
WBENC National WBE Certification 0534
Multiple state and county certifications available upon request.

Acknowledgements

With love and thanks to the amazing original members of western Pennsylvania's Ladies Who Brunch network: Gina Byerlein, Amy Criss, Mama Donna Criss, Monique DeMonaco, Danielle Dietrich, Carol Philp and Barb Smith. The support of our core tribe in business is an on-going and priceless personal gift.

Certify and Sell

Eternal gratitude for the extraordinary thoughtfulness and support of the Diversity Equity and Inclusion mentors, Heather Herndon Wright and Jay Sheldon Wesley.

The engagement with Chatham University and its Center for Women's Entrepreneurship gave us the foundation to educate diverse business owners. Special thanks are owed to Rebecca U. Harris and Anne Flynn Schlicht.

Sharing is caring! Thanks to the organizations and people who were kind enough to share their insights through the interview process.

We so appreciate Earl Mann who helped us understand and clarify our value.

Thank you to every Abator customer. Without you, there would be no business, no need for certification or the educational journey that led to this book.

Certifiers! Without your patience and guidance, the journey would have been incomplete.

To our brothers and sisters in the diverse community—we are family and, as such, hope to lift us all.

Each other, for the ability to work together in all phases of business and family life. Couldn't do it without you.

Bibliography

BasuMallick, C. (2020, 1 10). *Diversity and Inclusion Trends 2020*. Retrieved from hrtechnogist.com: https://www.hrtechnologist.com/articles/diversity/diversity-and-inclusion-trends-2020/

Billion Dollar Roundtable. (2010). *"Supplier Diversity Best Practices" Edited by M. V. Greene.* Dallas: MBM Custom Publications.

Bridges, J. (2020, 1 28). *Workplace Training*. Retrieved from Erverfi.com: https://everfi.com/blog/workplace-training/5-diversity-equity-and-inclusion-trends/

Burks, D. L. (2019, 5 27). Comcast, Director Supplier Diversity . (J. Peterson, Interviewer)

Christman, G. (2020, 1 15). President & CEO, Hunter International Recruiting. (J. Peterson, Interviewer)

Clark, C. C. (2018, 6 26). *Government Executive Management*. Retrieved from Government Executive: https://www.govexec.com/management/2018/06/watchdog-finds-flaws-certification-process-women-owned-small-businesses/149301/

Collection, E. P. (2020, 5 21). *Plight of Essential Workers*.
Retrieved from US National Library of Medicine:
https://www.ncbi.nlm.nih.gov/pmc/articles/PMC7241
973/

Congress. (1964, 7 2). *Title VII of the Civil Rights Act of 1964*.
Retrieved from U.S. Equal Employment Opportunity
Commission: https://www.eeoc.gov/statutes/title-vii-
civil-rights-act-1964

Congress. (1978, 10 24). H.R.11318 . *A bill to amend the Small
Business Act and the Small Business Investment Act of
1958*. Washington, DC:
https://www.congress.gov/bill/95th-congress/house-
bill/11318. Retrieved from
https://www.govinfo.gov/content/pkg/STATUTE-
92/pdf/STATUTE-92-Pg1757.pdf#page=4

Congress. (2002, 7 24). H. R. 3763. *Sarbanes-Oxley Act of
2002*. Washington, DC:
https://www.congress.gov/bill/107th-congress/house-
bill/3763.

Corona Virus-19. (2020, 7 24). Retrieved from CDC.gov:
https://www.cdc.gov/coronavirus/2019-
ncov/community/health-equity/race-

ethnicity.html?CDC_AA_refVal=https%3A%2F%2Fww
w.cdc.gov%2Fcoronavirus%2F2019-ncov%2Fneed-
extra-precautions%2Fracial-ethnic-minorities.html

Corporate Relations. (2019, 12 12). *National Business Inclusion Consortium*. Retrieved from National Gay & Lesbian Chamber of Commerce: https://www.nglcc.org/NBIC

Cotteleer, M. &. (2017, 12 18). *Deloitte Global Millennial Survey*. Retrieved from Deloitte.com: https://www2.deloitte.com/content/dam/Deloitte/glob al/Documents/About-Deloitte/gx-2018-millennial-survey-report.pdf

Crenshaw, K. (2019, 5 20). *Demarginalizing the Intersection of Race and Sex: A Black Feminist Critique of Antidiscrimination Doctrine, Feminist Theory and Antiracist Politics*. Retrieved from Vox: https://www.vox.com/the-highlight/2019/5/20/18542843/intersectionality-conservatism-law-race-gender-discrimination

Criss, A. (2019, 5 18). Amazon; Talent Supply Chain Staffing, Operations and Analytics. (J. Peterson, Interviewer)

Department of Defense. (2018, 12). *Report to Congress Section 889 ofthe FY 2018 NDAA Report on Defense Contracting Fraud* . Retrieved from Office of the Under Secretary of Defense for Acquisition and Sustainment : https://fas.org/man/eprint/contract-fraud.pdf

Dilger, R. J. (2019, 12 6). *Congressional Research Services.* Retrieved from crsreports: https://crsreports.congress.gov/product/pdf/R/R4086 0

Dockendorf, R. (2011, 2 10). *Yankton Daily Press & Dakotan News.* Retrieved from Yankton Daily Press & Dakotan: https://www.yankton.net/community/article_d05f2d0 6-0cfa-5c74-9411-d5ee67722f10.html

Executive Office of the President OMB. (2016, 8 8). *Uniited States Census Bureau.* Retrieved from North American Industry Classification System: https://www.census.gov/eos/www/naics/

Executive Office of the President OMB. (2017). *North American Industry Classification System.* Retrieved from US Census: https://www.census.gov/eos/www/naics/2017NAICS/ 2017_NAICS_Manual.pdf

Gulliver-Garcia, T. &. (2020, 8 18). *U.S. Civil Unrest.*
Retrieved from DisasterPhilanthropy.org:
https://disasterphilanthropy.org/disaster/u-s-civil-
unrest/

Hernandez, F. (2020, 1 15). Microsoft, Director Supplier
Diversity & Sustainability. (J. Peterson, Interviewer)

Insight Center for Community Economic Development. (2017,
1 1). *State Inclusive Business Program.* Retrieved from
Insight Center: https://insightcced.org/past-
archives/insight-networks/inbiz-the-inclusive-
business-initiative/state-inclusive-business-program-
overview-goals/

Johnson, L. B. (1965, 9 24). Executive Order 11246. *Equal
Employment Opportunity.* Washington, DC, US:
National Archives https://www.archives.gov/federal-
register/codification/executive-
order/11246.html#:~:text=11246%20of%20September
%2024%2C%201965%2C%20and%20by%20the%20rul
es%2C,with%20such%20rules%2C%20regulations%2C
%20and.

Juncker, Jean-Claude. (2014, 3 21). *Making socially
responsible procurement work.* Retrieved from EU

European Commission: https://ec.europa.eu/info/policies/public-procurement/support-tools-public-buyers/social-procurement_en

Kain, H. (2019, 9 9). Alom, Global Supply Chain Executive. (J. Peterson, Interviewer)

Kaufman, J. (2020, 6 15). *Diversity and Inclusion; Mindset Matters*. Retrieved from Forbes.com: https://www.forbes.com/sites/jonathankaufman/2020/06/15/mindset-matters-whats-next-for-diversity-and-inclusion-professionals-in-the-wake-of-civil-unrest/#f8ce2fa353d3

Kim, M. (2020, 1 28). *Awaken Blog*. Retrieved from Medium.com: https://medium.com/awaken-blog/top-10-diversity-equity-and-inclusion-trends-and-recommendations-2020-and-beyond-65c170725e4f

King, K. (2019, 12 12). NVBDC President. (J. Peterson, Interviewer)

Koprince, S. (2013, 3 8). *SmallGovCon Blog*. Retrieved from SmallGovCon: https://smallgovcon.com/debarment-

and-penalties/false-wosb-self-certifications-potentially-rampant-says-nasa-oig/

Koprince, S. (2020, 6 2). *SmallGovCon Blog*. Retrieved from SmallGovCon: https://smallgovcon.com/government-contracts-attorney/wosb-attorney/

Korkeoja, Juha. (2016, 7 18). *European Union Council 2745th Council Meeting*. Retrieved from European Union Council: https://ec.europa.eu/commission/presscorner/detail/en/PRES_06_217

Kutz, G. D. (2009, 12 16). *GAO Reports and Testimonies Service Disabled Veteran-Owned Small Business Program: Case Studies Show Fraud and Abuse Allowed Ineligible Firms to Obtain Millions of Dollars in Contracts*. Retrieved from US Government Accountability Office: https://www.gao.gov/products/GAO-10-306T

Lohm, M. (2019, 12 12). NaVOBA. (J. Peterson, Interviewer)

Mann, E. (2020, 1 13). President, OQ Point LLC. (J. Peterson, Interviewer)

McClain, P. "Joe". (2019, 5 30). Eaton Director, Supplier Diversity. (J. Peterson, Interviewer)

Minority Business Development Agency. (2019, 10 23). *Minority Business Development Agency History*. Retrieved from Minority Business Development Agency: https://www.mbda.gov/about/history

Mizer, B. C. (2016, 12 14). *DOJ Public Affairs News*. Retrieved from US Department of Justice Public Affairs: https://www.justice.gov/opa/pr/justice-department-recovers-over-47-billion-false-claims-act-cases-fiscal-year-2016

National Archives. (1920). *National Archives Exhibits*. Retrieved from National Archives: https://www.archives.gov/exhibits/featured-documents/amendment-19

National Minority Supplier Development Council. (2018, 1 20). *National Minority Supplier Development Council Facts and Figures*. Retrieved from National Minority Supplier Development Council: https://www.nmsdc.org/Facts-and-Figures.pdf

Nelson, J. (2020, 1 8). NGLCC Cofounder. (J. Peterson, Interviewer)

Nixon, R. M. (1969, 3 5). Exectuive Order 11458. *Prescribing Arrangements for Developing and Coordinating a National Program For Minority Business Enterprise.* Washington, DC: The American Presidency Project https://www.presidency.ucsb.edu/documents/executive-order-11458-prescribing-arrangements-for-developing-and-coordinating-national.

Nixon, R. M. (1969, 8 8). Executive Order 11478. *Equal employment opportunity in the Federal Government.* Washington, DC, United States: National Archives https://www.archives.gov/federal-register/codification/executive-order/11478.html.

Nixon, R. M. (1971, 10 13). Executive Order 11625. *Prescribing additional arrangements for developing and coordinating a national program for minority business enterprise.* Washington, DC, US: National Archives https://www.archives.gov/federal-register/codification/executive-order/11625.html.

O'Hara, N. (2020, 1 7). Executive, EMRCPR LLC. (J. Peterson, Interviewer)

Paonessa, T. (2020, 4 24). Owner, J.P. Investigative Group, Inc. (J. Peterson, Interviewer)

Parliment. (2000, 8 1). *UK Public General Acts*. Retrieved from Legislation Gov UK: https://www.legislation.gov.uk/ukpga/2000/22/pdfs/ ukpga_20000022_en.pdf

Peach, J. D. (1988, 11 30). *GAO Reports and Testimonies Assessing Fraud and Abuse in FHwA's Disadvantaged Business Enterprise Program*. Retrieved from US Government Accountability Office: https://www.gao.gov/products/RCED-89-26

Peterson, J. (2013, 3 25). Abator President/CEO. (S. o. Analyst, Interviewer)

Popular Pittsburgh. (2016, 2 25). *https://popularpittsburgh.com/pittsburghblackhistor y/*. Retrieved from https://popularpittsburgh.com.

Prince-Eason, P. (2020, 2 24). WBENC President. (J. Peterson, Interviewer)

Reagan, R. W. (1983, 7 14). Executive Order 12432. *Minority business enterprise development*. Washington, DC:

National Archives https://www.archives.gov/federal-register/codification/executive-order/12432.html.

Richey, W. (1985, 9 30). Racketeering Act turns on corporations. *Christian Science Monitor*. Washington, DC: https://www.csmonitor.com/1985/0930/arack.html.

Richey, W. (2017, 6 21). *Christian Science Monitor*. Retrieved from Christian Science Monitor: https://www.csmonitor.com/USA/Society/2017/0621/An-epic-case-of-medical-fraud-and-the-agent-who-cracked-it

Robinson, B. (2019, 10 14). Owner, VIVA Consulting Group. (J. Peterson, Interviewer)

Sault, S. (2020, 6 24). *World Economic Forum Agenda*. Retrieved from World Economic Forum: https://www.weforum.org/agenda/2020/06/companies-fighting-systemic-racism-business-community-black-lives-matter/

Saylor Academy. (2012, 1 1). *Business 209: Organizational Behavior IBM Case Study*. Retrieved from Saylor Academy:

https://saylordotorg.github.io/text_organizational-behavior-v1.1/s06-05-managing-diversity-for-success.html

SBA Office of Policy, Planning and Liaison. (2020, 9 18). *Government Wide Performance.* Retrieved from SBA.gov: https://www.sba.gov/sites/default/files/2020-09/G-W.pdf

Scifers, J. (2020, 4 24). President, Scigon. (J. Peterson, Interviewer)

Shapiro, J. (2020, 6 9). *Special Series: The Corona Virus.* Retrieved from NPR.org: https://www.npr.org/2020/06/09/872401607/covid-19-infections-and-deaths-are-higher-among-those-with-intellectual-disabili

Shoraka, J. (2014, 10 8). *Women-Owned Small Business Program Certifier Oversight and Additional Eligibility Controls Are Needed.* Retrieved from Governement Accountability Office: https://www.gao.gov/assets/670/666431.pdf

Small Business Administration (SBA). (2019, 8 19). *SBA Size Standards Tool*. Retrieved from SBA.gov: https://www.sba.gov/document/support--table-size-standards

Swenor, B. (2020, 4 23). *Johns Hopkins University HUB*. Retrieved from jhu.edu: https://hub.jhu.edu/2020/04/23/how-covid-19-affects-people-with-disabilities/

Taylor, R. (2019, 10 17). CEO, ImbuTec. (J. Peterson, Interviewer)

The Report of the President's Committee on Civil Rights. (1946, 12 5). *To Secure These Rights*. Retrieved from Harry S. Truman Library & Museum: https://www.trumanlibrary.gov/library/to-secure-these-rights

Turcotte, C. (2019, 10 14). Disability:IN Certification Manager. (J. Peterson, Interviewer)

US Government. (2019, 12 19). *United States Office of Government Ethics*. Retrieved from Gifts and Payments:

https://www.oge.gov/web/oge.nsf/Gifts%20and%20Pa
yments

Vowels, P. S. (2017). *Hacking Supplier Diversity: Cracking the Code for the Business Case: Revenue Generation, Economic Impact, ROI*. The Institute for Thought Diversity.

Vowels, P. S. (n.d.). *Hacking Supplier Diversity: Cracking the Code for the Business* .

Wade, C. (1982, 4 10). "Contractors Seek Role in Kane Job". *Pittsburgh Post Gazette*, p. 3.

WBENC. (1992, 12 11). *Women's Enterprise Presents: Business America's Game - Where are the Women?* Retrieved from Abator's Youtube Channel: https://www.youtube.com/watch?v=k0AIH9tyqlY

Wesley, J. S. (2019, 5 27). Lumen Technologies Global Corporate Supplier Diversity Office. (J. Peterson, Interviewer)

Wright, H. H. (2020, 9 16). Vistra Director, Supply Chain Diversity. (J. Peterson, Interviewer)

Wright, H. H. (2020, 1 15). Vistra Director, Supply Chain Diversity. (J. Peterson, Interviewer)

Zook, J. (2019, 8 27). President & CEO, Trattativa Meeting & Event Solutions International. (J. Peterson, Interviewer)

About the Authors

Joanne E. Peterson

When Joanne Peterson started Abator in 1983, very few women-owned technology firms existed. Today, in addition to her passion for helping clients achieve intelligent use of information, Peterson co-authors a blog for diverse business owners, provides technical assistance through Chatham's Center for Women's Entrepreneurship, served on PowerLink's board, and volunteers via WBEC East/WBENC.

Abator is a multi-faceted traditional consultancy supporting government and commercial clients building engagement teams that develop solutions to meet frequent business, legislative or critical regulatory reporting challenges. Its product lines include 360-Access.com and GetDiversityCertified.com.

Peterson began her consulting career with Cutler Williams in Dallas, Texas, followed by a stint with Allen Services and Consultant Systems before establishing Abator in Pittsburgh, Pa. She grew the business, negotiating contracts with major multi-national companies and state governments in developing custom software application systems.

Peterson is an alumna of WBENC's first Dartmouth College Tuck School of Business executive management training program (Hanover, NH), Chatham University's economics and management program (Pittsburgh, Pa.), and Grahm Junior College's mass communications program (Boston, Mass.).

Awards and Other Recognition:

- PowerLink 25th Anniversary Honoree (2017)
- Chatham University's Cornerstone Award in Information Technology (2016)
- SBA 8(a) Program Graduate 2013
- Women's Business Enterprise Council (WBEC East)/WBENC's Shining Star (2006 and 2018)
- In *Technology* "Women CEOs: Why So Few in the Region's High-Tech Community" (1994)
- *Inc. Magazine's* Entrepreneur of the Year Finalist (1989, 1990)

Marian E. Neilson

Marian E. Neilson is a 2003 graduate of Chatham University (Pittsburgh, Pa.) with a BA in English, minoring in history, and a graduate of the SBA's emerging leaders program. She is a third-generation owner of Abator, founded by her mother when Neilson was just two. She grew up playing at tasks for which she is now responsible.

In addition to the financial and human resources functions she performs for the company, Neilson provides primary support for Abator's GetDiversityCertified.com service designed to assist diverse business owners on the path to diversity certification. Having documented eligibility requirements for numerous federal, state, city/county, and third-party certifying organizations in the United States, she has unparalleled knowledge of certification processes with a deep commitment to helping others successfully navigate them.

Neilson assisted in developing Abator's Am I Certifiable and RFP Bootcamp courses and training materials, and co-leads them with Peterson. She co-authors a blog for diverse business owners, provides technical assistance through Chatham's WBC, is a notary, and is a self-proclaimed WBE Wrangler, organizing the Ladies Who Brunch in western Pennsylvania.

She volunteers through WBEC East, a WBENC regional partner organization.

www.ingramcontent.com/pod-product-compliance
Lightning Source LLC
Chambersburg PA
CBHW052122270326
41930CB00012B/2718